Android UI Development with Jetpack Compose

Bring declarative and native UIs to life quickly and easily on Android using Jetpack Compose

Thomas Künneth

BIRMINGHAM—MUMBAI

Android UI Development with Jetpack Compose

Copyright © 2022 Packt Publishing

Group Product Manager: Rohit Rajkumar
Publishing Product Manager: Shalita Aranha
Senior Editor: Hayden Edwards
Content Development Editor: Abhishek Jadhav
Technical Editor: Joseph Aloocaran
Copy Editor: Safis Editing
Project Coordinator: Rashika Ba
Proofreader: Safis Editing
Indexer: Tejal Daruwale Soni
Production Designer: Shyam Sundar Korumili
Marketing Coordinator: Elizabeth Varghese

First published: February 2022

Production reference: 2140222

Published by Packt Publishing Ltd.
Livery Place
35 Livery Street
Birmingham
B3 2PB, UK.

ISBN 978-1-80181-216-0

www.packt.com

To my beloved wife, Moni. You are the light of my life.

To the Android developer community for driving the Android ecosystem, for inspiration, insights, and for support.

To all my friends and supporters.

To the fine people that contributed to and supported this book.

– Thomas Künneth

Contributors

About the author

Thomas Künneth is a Google Developer Expert for Android and has been a speaker and panelist at multiple international conferences about Android. His first Android app, published in 2010, has more than 100,000 downloads. Currently, Thomas works as a principal consultant and head of mobile at MATHEMA GmbH and has experience as a software architect and Android developer. He has authored countless articles as well as one of the top-selling German Android books (currently in its sixth edition). He has also frequently contributed to various open source projects.

About the reviewers

Paul Blundell is an accomplished Android developer who has designed, programmed, engineered, architected, tested, and shipped hundreds of apps, with hundreds of millions in downloads over a 12-year Android career. He's worked at notable companies such as Twitter, M-KOPA, Novoda, AutoTrader, and Thales UK. He is also the published author of the Android testing book *Learning Android Application Testing* and a renowned Google Developer Expert and blogger, tweeting from `@blundell_apps`.

Mitchell Wong Ho was born in Johannesburg, South Africa, where he completed his national diploma in electrical engineering. Mitchell's software development career started on embedded systems and then moved to Microsoft desktop/server applications. Mitchell has been programming in Java since 2000 on J2ME, JEE, desktop, and Android applications, and has more recently been developing cross-platform mobile apps using React Native and Flutter.

The Peer Reviewers

The following individuals have helped in peer-reviewing the book:

- **Can Yumusak**
- **Jomar Tigcal**
- **Yev Kanivets**
- **Guilherme Delgado**
- **Adit Lal**

Table of Contents

3
Exploring the Key Principles of Compose

Part 2: Building User Interfaces

4
Laying Out UI Elements

5
Managing the State of Your Composable Functions

6

Putting Pieces Together

7

Tips, Tricks, and Best Practices

Part 3: Advanced Topics

8

Working with Animations

Preface

Jetpack Compose is Android's new framework for building fast, beautiful, and reliable native user interfaces. It simplifies and significantly accelerates UI development on Android using the declarative approach. This book will help developers to get hands-on with Jetpack Compose and adopt a modern way of building Android applications. The book is not an introduction to Android development, but it will build on your knowledge of how Android apps are developed.

Complete with hands-on tutorials and projects, this easy-to-follow guide will get you up to speed with the fundamentals of Jetpack Compose, such as state hoisting, unidirectional data flow, and composition over inheritance, and help you build your own Android apps using Compose. You'll also cover concepts such as testing, animation, and interoperability with the existing Android UI toolkit.

By the end of the book, you'll be able to write your own Android apps using Jetpack Compose.

Who this book is for

This book is for any mobile app developer looking to understand the fundamentals of the new Jetpack Compose framework and the benefits of native development. A solid understanding of Android app development, along with some knowledge of the Kotlin programming language, will be beneficial. Basic programming knowledge is necessary to grasp the concepts covered in this book effectively.

What this book covers

Chapter 1, Building Your First Compose App, shows you how to build your first Compose app. Also, important key ideas such as composable functions and using previews are introduced. It is important to whet the appetite with early success, so we'll build, preview, and run composable functions before digging too deep into details.

Chapter 2, Understanding the Declarative Paradigm, explains how this was done before, and what the issues with the *old* approach are. Also, you'll an idea how composables are different to Views, and why this is both important and beneficial.

Chapter 3, *Exploring the Key Principles of Compose*, introduces the key principles that Jetpack Compose relies on. This knowledge is essential for writing well-behaved Compose apps.

Chapter 4, *Laying Out UI Elements*, introduces you to some of the existing layouts. It also shows you how to implement custom layouts. These are needed if the built-in layouts cannot provide the required distribution of UI elements onscreen.

Chapter 5, *Managing the State of Your Composable Functions*, takes a look at how Jetpack Compose uses state. State is app data that may change over time. Composable functions display and modify state. Jetpack Compose is based upon a small set of principles regarding how to use state. This chapter acquaints you with these principles.

Chapter 6, *Putting Pieces Together*, catches up on previously learned concepts and brings them together in one app. Seeing concepts in real code helps understand them and makes it easier to reuse them in your own programs.

Chapter 7, *Tips, Tricks, and Best Practices*, provides best practices when using Compose. These will include topics such as persisting and retrieving state and using so-called side effects. The chapter also shows things to avoid, such as having heavy computations inside a composable function.

Chapter 8, *Working with Animations*, introduces all relevant APIs. Animations and transitions make apps really shine. Jetpack Compose simplifies the process of adding animation effects greatly over the old View-based approach.

Chapter 9, *Exploring Interoperability APIs*, discusses strategies to combine declarative and imperative approaches in one app and offers a migration strategy to painlessly update existing UIs to Jetpack Compose.

Chapter 10, *Testing and Debugging Compose Apps*, introduces basic testing scenarios for Compose apps. Testing the user interface of a Compose app works differently than testing a view-based UI. Compose uses a more declarative approach to testing.

Chapter 11, *Conclusion and Next Steps*, wraps up the book in directing you to things you can try next. Also, the chapter attempts to guess what the future will hold for Jetpack Compose and looks into neighboring platforms and how you can benefit from your knowledge on them.

To get the most out of this book

You will need at least Android Studio Arctic Fox or later. To run the sample apps, you also require a configured Android emulator or a real device. Jetpack Compose works on platforms with an API level of 21 or greater.

Software/hardware covered in the book	Operating system requirements
Android Studio Arctic Fox	Windows, macOS, or Linux

If you are using the digital version of this book, we advise you to type the code yourself or access the code from the book's GitHub repository (a link is available in the next section). Doing so will help you avoid any potential errors related to the copying and pasting of code.

Download the example code files

You can download the example code files for this book from GitHub at `https://github.com/PacktPublishing/Android-UI-Development-with-Jetpack-Compose`. If there's an update to the code, it will be updated in the GitHub repository.

We also have other code bundles from our rich catalog of books and videos available at `https://github.com/PacktPublishing/`. Check them out!

Download the color images

We also provide a PDF file that has color images of the screenshots and diagrams used in this book. You can download it here: `https://static.packt-cdn.com/downloads/9781801812160_ColorImages.pdf`.

Conventions used

There are a number of text conventions used throughout this book.

`Code in text`: Indicates code words in text, database table names, folder names, filenames, file extensions, pathnames, dummy URLs, user input, and Twitter handles. Here is an example: "If you have already cloned or downloaded the repository of this book, its project folder is located inside `chapter_01`."

A block of code is set as follows:

```
@Composable

fun Greeting(name: String) {

    Text(
```

```
        text = stringResource(id = R.string.hello, name),

        textAlign = TextAlign.Center,

        style = MaterialTheme.typography.subtitle1

    )

}
```

When we wish to draw your attention to a particular part of a code block, the relevant lines or items are set in bold:

```
TextField(

    value = name.value,

    onValueChange = {

        name.value = it

    },
```

Bold: Indicates a new term, an important word, or words that you see onscreen. For instance, words in menus or dialog boxes appear in **bold**. Here is an example: "After you have entered your name and clicked on the **Done** button, you will see a greeting message."

> **Tips or important notes**
> Appear like this.

Get in touch

Feedback from our readers is always welcome.

General feedback: If you have questions about any aspect of this book, email us at customercare@packtpub.com and mention the book title in the subject of your message.

Errata: Although we have taken every care to ensure the accuracy of our content, mistakes do happen. If you have found a mistake in this book, we would be grateful if you would report this to us. Please visit www.packtpub.com/support/errata and fill in the form.

Piracy: If you come across any illegal copies of our works in any form on the internet, we would be grateful if you would provide us with the location address or website name. Please contact us at copyright@packt.com with a link to the material.

If you are interested in becoming an author: If there is a topic that you have expertise in and you are interested in either writing or contributing to a book, please visit authors.packtpub.com.

Share Your Thoughts

Once you've read *Android UI Development with Jetpack Compose*, we'd love to hear your thoughts! Scan the QR code below to go straight to the Amazon review page for this book and share your feedback.

https://www.amazon.in/review/create-review/error?asin=1801812160

Your review is important to us and the tech community and will help us make sure we're delivering excellent quality content.

Part 1: Fundamentals of Jetpack Compose

In this part, you will get to know important basic concepts of Jetpack Compose. Their understanding is necessary to write well-behaving Compose apps.

We will cover the following chapters in this section:

- *Chapter 1, Building Your First Compose App*
- *Chapter 2, Understanding the Declarative Paradigm*
- *Chapter 3, Exploring the Key Principles of Compose*

1
Building Your First Compose App

When Android was introduced more than 10 years ago, it quickly gained popularity among developers because it was incredibly easy to write apps. All you had to do was define the user interface (UI) in an XML file and connect it to your *activity*. This worked flawlessly because apps were small and developers needed to support just a handful of devices.

So much has changed since then.

With every new platform version, Android gained new features. Through the years, device manufacturers introduced thousands of devices with different screen sizes, pixel densities, and form factors. While Google did its best to keep the Android *view* system comprehendible, the complexity of apps increased significantly; basic tasks such as implementing scrolling lists or animations require lots of boilerplate code.

It turned out that these problems were not specific to Android. Other platforms and operating systems faced them as well. Most issues stem from how UI toolkits used to work; they follow a so-called **imperative approach** (which I will explain in *Chapter 2, Understanding the Declarative Paradigm*). The solution was a paradigm shift. The web framework React was the first to popularize a declarative approach. Other platforms and frameworks (for example, Flutter and SwiftUI) followed.

Jetpack Compose is Google's declarative UI framework for Android. It dramatically simplifies the creation of UIs. As you will surely agree after reading this book, using Jetpack Compose is both easy and fun. But before we dive in, please note that Jetpack Compose is Kotlin-only. This means that all your Compose code will have to be written in Kotlin. To follow this book, you should have a basic understanding of the Kotlin syntax and the functional programming model. If you want to learn more about these topics, please refer to the *Further reading* section at the end of this chapter.

This chapter covers three main topics:

- Saying hello to composable functions
- Using the preview
- Running a Compose app

I will explain how to build a simple UI with Jetpack Compose. Next, you will learn to use the **preview** feature in Android Studio and how to run a Compose app. By the end of this chapter, you will have a basic understanding of how composable functions work, how they are integrated into your app, and how your project must be configured in order to use Jetpack Compose.

Technical requirements

All the code files for this chapter can be found on GitHub at `https://github.com/PacktPublishing/Android-UI-Development-with-Jetpack-Compose/tree/main/chapter_01`. Please download the zipped version or clone the repository to an arbitrary location on your computer. The projects require at least Android Studio Arctic Fox. You can download the latest version at `https://developer.android.com/studio`. Please follow the detailed installation instructions at `https://developer.android.com/studio/install`.

To open this book's project, launch Android Studio, click the **Open** button in the upper-right area of the **Welcome to Android Studio** window, and select the base directory of the project in the folder selection dialog. Please make sure to not open the base directory of the repository, because Android Studio would not recognize the projects. Instead, you must pick the directory that contains the project you want to work with.

To run a sample app, you need a real device or the Android Emulator. Please make sure that developer options and USB debugging are enabled on the real device, and that the device is connected to your development machine via USB or WLAN. Please follow the instructions at `https://developer.android.com/studio/debug/dev-options`. You can also set up the Android Emulator. You can find detailed instructions at `https://developer.android.com/studio/run/emulator`.

Saying hello to composable functions

As you will see shortly, composable functions are the essential building blocks of Compose apps; these elements make up the UI.

To take a first look at them, I will walk you through a simple app called **Hello** (*Figure 1.1*). If you have already cloned or downloaded the repository of this book, its project folder is located inside `chapter_01`. Otherwise, please do so now. To follow this section, open the project in Android Studio and open `MainActivity.kt`. The use case of our first Compose app is very simple. After you have entered your name and clicked on the **Done** button, you will see a greeting message:

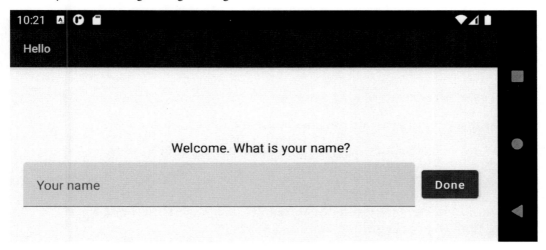

Figure 1.1 – The Hello app

Conceptually, the app consists of the following:

- The welcome text
- A row with an `EditText` equivalent and a button
- A greeting message

Let's take a look at how to create the app.

Showing a welcome text

Let's start with the welcome text, our first composable function:

```
@Composable
fun Welcome() {
    Text(
```

```
        text = stringResource(id = R.string.welcome),
        style = MaterialTheme.typography.subtitle1
    )
}
```

Composable functions can be easily identified by the @Composable annotation. They do not need to have a particular return type but instead emit UI elements. This is usually done by invoking other composables (for the sake of brevity, I will sometimes omit the word "function"). *Chapter 3, Exploring the Key Principles of Compose*, will cover this in greater detail.

In this example, Welcome() summons a text. Text() is a built-in composable function and belongs to the androidx.compose.material package.

To invoke Text() just by its name, you need to import it:

```
import androidx.compose.material.Text
```

Please note that you can save import lines by using the * wildcard.

To use Text() and other Material Design elements, your build.gradle file must include an implementation dependency to androidx.compose.material:material.

Looking back at the welcome text code, the Text() composable inside Welcome() is configured through two parameters, text and style.

The first, text, specifies what text will be displayed. R.string may look familiar; it refers to definitions inside the strings.xml files. Just like in view-based apps, you define text for UI elements there. stringResource() is a predefined composable function. It belongs to the androidx.compose.ui.res package.

The style parameter modifies the visual appearance of a text. In this case, the output will look like a subtitle. I will show you how to create your own themes in *Chapter 6, Putting Pieces Together*.

The next composable looks quite similar. Can you spot the differences?

```
@Composable
fun Greeting(name: String) {
    Text(
        text = stringResource(id = R.string.hello, name),
        textAlign = TextAlign.Center,
        style = MaterialTheme.typography.subtitle1
```

```
    )
}
```

Here, `stringResource()` receives an additional parameter. This is very convenient for replacing placeholders with actual texts. The string is defined in `strings.xml`, as follows:

```
<string name="hello">Hello, %1$s.\nNice to meet you.</string>
```

The `textAlign` parameter specifies how text is positioned horizontally. Here, each line is centered.

Using rows, text fields, and buttons

Next, let's turn to the text input field (**Your name**) and the **Done** button, which both appear on the same row. This is a very common pattern, therefore Jetpack Compose provides a composable named `Row()`, which belongs to the `androidx.compose.foundation.layout` package. Just like all composable functions, `Row()` can receive a comma-separated list of parameters inside `( )` and its children are put inside curly braces:

```
@Composable
fun TextAndButton(name: MutableState<String>,
                  nameEntered: MutableState<Boolean>) {
    Row(modifier = Modifier.padding(top = 8.dp)) {
        ...
    }
}
```

`TextAndButton()` requires two parameters, `name` and `nameEntered`. You will see what they are used for in the *Showing a greeting message* section. For now, please ignore their `MutableState` type.

`Row()` receives a parameter called `modifier`. Modifiers are a key technique in Jetpack Compose to influence both the look and behavior of composable functions. I will explain them in greater detail in *Chapter 3, Exploring the Key Principles of Compose*.

`padding(top = 8.dp)` means that the row will have a padding of eight density-independent pixels (`.dp`) at its upper side, thus separating itself from the welcome message above it.

Now, we will look at the text input field, which allows the user to enter a name:

```
TextField(
  value = name.value,
  onValueChange = {
    name.value = it
  },
  placeholder = {
    Text(text = stringResource(id = R.string.hint))
  },
  modifier = Modifier
    .alignByBaseline()
    .weight(1.0F),
  singleLine = true,
  keyboardOptions = KeyboardOptions(
    autoCorrect = false,
    capitalization = KeyboardCapitalization.Words,
  ),
  keyboardActions = KeyboardActions(onAny = {
    nameEntered.value = true
  })
)
```

TextField() belongs to the androidx.compose.material package. The composable can receive quite a few arguments; most of them are optional, though. Please note that the previous code fragment uses both the name and nameEntered parameters, which are passed to TextAndButton(). Their type is MutableState. MutableState objects carry changeable values, which you access as name.value or nameEntered.value.

The value parameter of a TextField() composable receives the current value of the text input field, for example, text that has already been input. onValueChange is invoked when changes to the text occur (if the user enters or deletes something). But why is name.value used in both places? I will answer this question in the *Showing a greeting message* section.

> **Recomposition**
>
> Certain types trigger a so-called recomposition. For now, think of this as repainting an associated composable. `MutableState` is such a type. If we change its value, the `TextField()` composable is redrawn or repainted. Please note that both terms are not entirely correct. We will cover recomposition in *Chapter 3, Exploring the Key Principles of Compose.*

Let's briefly look at the remaining code. With `alignByBaseline()`, we can nicely align the baselines of other composable functions in a particular `Row()`. `placeholder` contains the text that is shown until the user has entered something. `singleLine` controls whether the user can enter multiple lines of text. Finally, `keyboardOptions` and `keyboardActions` describe the behavior of the onscreen keyboard. For example, certain actions will set `nameEntered.value` to `true`. I will show you soon why we do this.

However, we need to take a look at the `Button()` composable first. It also belongs to the `androidx.compose.material` package:

```
Button(modifier = Modifier
    .alignByBaseline()
    .padding(8.dp),
    onClick = {
        nameEntered.value = true
    }) {
    Text(text = stringResource(id = R.string.done))
}
```

Some things will already look familiar. For example, we call `alignByBaseline()` to align the baseline of the button with the text input field, and we apply a padding of eight density-independent pixels to all sides of the button using `padding()`. Now, `onClick()` specifies what to do when the button is clicked. Here, too, we set `nameEntered.value` to `true`. The next composable function, `Hello()`, finally shows you why this is done.

Showing a greeting message

`Hello()` emits `Box()`, which (depending on `nameEntered.value`) contains either the `Greeting()` or a `Column()` composable that, in turn, includes `Welcome()` and `TextAndButton()`. The `Column()` composable is quite similar to `Row()` but arranges its siblings vertically. Like the latter one and `Box()`, it belongs to the `androidx. compose.foundation.layout` package. `Box()` can contain one or more children. They are positioned inside the box according to the `contentAlignment` parameter. We will be exploring this in greater detail in the *Combining basic building blocks* section of *Chapter 4, Laying Out UI Elements*:

```
@Composable
fun Hello() {
  val name = remember { mutableStateOf("") }
  val nameEntered = remember { mutableStateOf(false) }
  Box(
    modifier = Modifier
      .fillMaxSize()
      .padding(16.dp),
    contentAlignment = Alignment.Center
  ) {
    if (nameEntered.value) {
      Greeting(name.value)
    } else {
      Column(horizontalAlignment =
            Alignment.CenterHorizontally) {
        Welcome()
        TextAndButton(name, nameEntered)
      }
    }
  }
}
```

Have you noticed `remember` and `mutableStateOf`? Both are very important for creating and maintaining state. Generally speaking, state in an app refers to a value that can change over time. While this also applies to domain data (for example, the result of a web service call), state usually refers to something being displayed or used by a UI element. If a composable function has (or relies on) state, it is recomposed (for now, repainted or redrawn) when that state changes. To get an idea of what this means, recall this composable:

```
@Composable
fun Welcome() {
    Text(
        text = stringResource(id = R.string.welcome),
        style = MaterialTheme.typography.subtitle1
    )
}
```

`Welcome()` is said to be stateless; all values that might trigger a recomposition remain the same for the time being. `Hello()`, on the other hand, is stateful, because it uses the `name` and `nameEntered` variables. They change over time. This may not be obvious if you look at the source code of `Hello()`. Please recall that both `name` and `nameEntered` are passed to `TextAndButton()` and modified there.

Do you recall that in the previous section I promised to explain why `name.value` is used in two places, providing the text to display and receiving changes after the user has entered something? This is a common pattern often used with states; `Hello()` creates and remembers state by invoking `mutableStateOf()` and `remember`. And it passes state to another composable (`TextAndButton()`), which is called **state hoisting**. You will learn more about this in *Chapter 5, Managing the State of Your Composable Functions*.

So far, you have seen the source code of quite a few composable functions but not their output. Android Studio has a very important feature called **Compose preview**. It allows you to view a composable function without running the app. In the next section, I will show you how to use this feature.

Using the preview

The upper-right corner of the Android Studio code editor contains three buttons, **Code**, **Split**, and **Design** (*Figure 1.2*):

Figure 1.2 – Compose preview (Split mode)

They switch between the following different display modes:

- Code only
- Code and preview
- Preview only

To use the Compose preview, your composable functions must contain an additional annotation, @Preview, which belongs to the androidx.compose.ui.tooling. preview package. This requires an implementation dependency to androidx. compose.ui:ui-tooling-preview in your build.gradle file.

Unfortunately, if you try to add @Preview to Greeting(), you will see an error message like this:

```
Composable functions with non-default parameters are not
supported in Preview unless they are annotated with
@PreviewParameter.
```

So, how can you preview composables that take parameters?

Preview parameters

The most obvious solution is a wrapper composable:

```
@Composable
@Preview
fun GreetingWrapper() {
```

```
        Greeting("Jetpack Compose")
}
```

This means that you write another composable function that takes no parameters but invokes your existing one and provides the required parameter (in my example, a text). Depending on how many composable functions your source file contains, you might be creating quite a lot of boilerplate code. The wrappers don't add value besides enabling the preview.

Fortunately, there are other options. You can, for example, add default values to your composable:

```
@Composable
fun AltGreeting(name: String = "Jetpack Compose") {
```

While this looks less hacky, it alters how your composable functions can be invoked (that is, without passing a parameter). This may not be desirable if you had a reason for not defining a default value in the first place.

With @PreviewParameter, you can pass values to a composable that affect only the preview. Unfortunately, this is a little verbose, though, because you need to write a new class:

```
class HelloProvider : PreviewParameterProvider<String> {
    override val values: Sequence<String>
        get() = listOf("PreviewParameterProvider").asSequence()
}
```

The class must extend androidx.compose.ui.tooling.preview. PreviewParameterProvider because it will provide a parameter for the preview. Now, you can annotate the parameter of the composable with @PreviewParameter and pass your new class:

```
@Composable
@Preview
fun AltGreeting2(@PreviewParameter(HelloProvider::class)
            name: String) {
```

In a way, you are creating boilerplate code, too. So, which method you choose in the end is a matter of personal taste. The @Preview annotation can receive quite a few parameters. They modify the visual appearance of the preview. Let's explore some of them.

Configuring previews

You can set a background color for a preview using `backgroundColor =`. The value is a `Long` type and represents an ARGB color. Please make sure to also set `showBackground` to `true`. The following snippet will produce a solid red background:

```
@Preview(showBackground = true, backgroundColor =
        0xffff0000)
```

By default, preview dimensions are chosen automatically. If you want to set them explicitly, you can pass `heightDp` and `widthDp`:

```
@Composable
@Preview(widthDp = 100, heightDp = 100)
fun Welcome() {
  Text(
    text = stringResource(id = R.string.welcome),
    style = MaterialTheme.typography.subtitle1
  )
}
```

Figure 1.3 shows the result. Both values are interpreted as density-independent pixels, so you don't need to add `.dp` as you would do inside your composable function.

Figure 1.3 – Setting the width and height of a preview

To test different user locales, you can add the `locale` parameter. If, for example, your app contains German strings inside `values-de-rDE`, you can use them by adding the following:

```
@Preview(locale = "de-rDE")
```

The string matches the directory name after `values-`. Please recall that the directory is created by Android Studio if you add a language in the Translations Editor.

If you want to display the status and action bars, you can achieve this with
showSystemUi:

```
@Preview(showSystemUi = true)
```

To get an idea of how your composables react to different form factors, aspect ratios,
and pixel densities, you can utilize the device parameter. It takes a string. Pass
one of the values from Devices, for example, Devices.PIXEL_C or Devices.
AUTOMOTIVE_1024p.

In this section, you have seen how to configure a preview. Next, I will introduce you to
preview groups. They are very handy if your source code file contains more than a few
composable functions that you want to preview.

Grouping previews

Android Studio shows composable functions with a @Preview annotation in the order
of their appearance in the source code. You can choose between **Vertical Layout** and **Grid
Layout** (*Figure 1.4*):

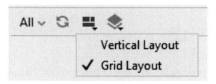

Figure 1.4 – Switching between Vertical Layout and Grid Layout

Depending on the number of your composables, the preview pane may at some point
feel crowded. If this is the case, just put your composables into different groups by adding
a group parameter:

```
@Preview(group = "my-group-1")
```

You can then show either all composable functions or just those that belong to a particular
group (*Figure 1.5*):

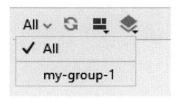

Figure 1.5 – Switching between groups

So far, I have shown you what the source code of composable functions looks like and how you can preview them inside Android Studio. In the next section, we will execute a composable on the Android Emulator or a real device, and you will learn how to connect composable functions to the other parts of an app. But before that, here is one more tip:

> **Export a Preview as an Image**
> If you click on a Compose preview with the secondary mouse button, you will see a small pop-up menu. Select **Copy Image** to put a bitmap of the preview on the system clipboard. Most graphics applications allow you to paste it into a new document.

Running a Compose app

If you want to see how a composable function looks and feels on the Android Emulator or a real device, you have two options:

- Deploying a composable function
- Running the app

The first option is useful if you want to focus on a particular composable rather than the whole app. Also, the time needed to deploy a composable may be significantly shorter than deploying a complete app (depending on the app size). So, let's start with this one.

Deploying a composable function

To deploy a composable function to a real device or the Android Emulator, click on the **Deploy Preview** button, which is a small image in the upper-right corner of a preview (*Figure 1.6*):

Figure 1.6 – Deploying a composable function

This will automatically create new launch configurations (*Figure 1.7*):

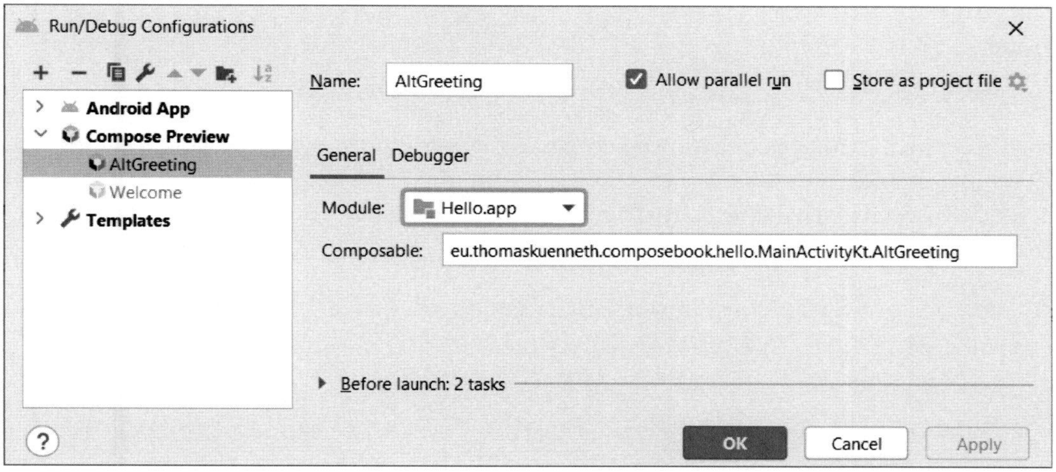

Figure 1.7 – Launch configurations representing Compose previews

You can modify or delete Compose preview configurations in the **Run/Debug Configurations** dialog. To access them, open the **Compose Preview** node. Then you can, for example, change its name or deny parallel runs by unchecking **Allow parallel run**.

The goal of this chapter is to deploy and run your first Compose app on a real device or the Android Emulator. You are almost there; in the next section, I will show you how to embed composable functions in an activity, which is a prerequisite. You will finally be running the app in the *Pressing the play button* section.

Using composable functions in activities

Activities have been one of the basic building blocks of Android apps since the first platform version. Practically every app has at least one activity. They are configured in the manifest file. To launch an activity from the home screen, the corresponding entry looks like this:

```
...
<activity
  android:name=".MainActivity"
  android:exported="true"
  android:label="@string/app_name">
  <intent-filter>
    <action android:name="android.intent.action.MAIN" />
    <category
```

```
        android:name="android.intent.category.LAUNCHER" />
    </intent-filter>
</activity>
...
```

This is still true for Compose apps. An activity that wishes to show composable functions is set up just like one that inflates a traditional layout file. But what does its source code look like? The main activity of the `Hello` app is called `MainActivity`, shown in the next code block:

```
class MainActivity : ComponentActivity() {
    override fun onCreate(savedInstanceState: Bundle?) {
        super.onCreate(savedInstanceState)
        setContent {
            Hello()
        }
    }
}
```

As you can see, it is very short. The UI (the `Hello()` composable function) is displayed by invoking a function called `setContent`, which is an extension function to `androidx.activity.ComponentActivity` and belongs to the `androidx.activity.compose` package.

To render composables, your activity must extend either `ComponentActivity` or another class that has `ComponentActivity` as its direct or indirect ancestor. This is the case for `androidx.fragment.app.FragmentActivity` and `androidx.appcompat.app.AppCompatActivity`.

This is an important difference; while Compose apps invoke `setContent()`, View-based apps call `setContentView()` and pass either the ID of a layout (`R.layout.activity_main`) or the root view itself (which is usually obtained through some binding mechanism). Let's see how the older mechanism works. The following code snippet is taken from one of my open source apps (you can find it on GitHub at `https://github.com/MATHEMA-GmbH/TKWeek` but it won't be discussed any further in this book):

```
class TKWeekActivity : TKWeekBaseActivity() {

    private var backing: TkweekBinding? = null
    private val binding get() = backing!!
```

```
override fun onCreate(savedInstanceState: Bundle?) {
  super.onCreate(savedInstanceState)
  backing = TkweekBinding.inflate(layoutInflater, null,
          false)
  setContentView(binding.root)
  ...
```

If you compare both approaches, a striking difference is that with Jetpack Compose, there is no need for maintaining references to the UI component tree or individual elements of it. I will explain in *Chapter 2, Understanding the Declarative Paradigm*, why this leads to code that is easily maintainable and less error-prone.

Let's now return to `setContent()`. It receives two parameters, a `parent` (which can be `null`) and the `content` (the UI). The `parent` is an instance of `androidx.compose.runtime.CompositionContext`. It is used to logically link together two compositions. This is an advanced topic that I will be discussing in *Chapter 3, Exploring the Key Principles of Compose*.

> **Important Note**
>
> Have you noticed that `MainActivity` does not contain any composable functions? They do not need to be part of a class. In fact, you should implement them as top-level functions whenever possible. Jetpack Compose provides alternative means to access `android.content.Context`. You have already seen the `stringResource()` composable function, which is a replacement for `getString()`.

Now that you have seen how to embed composable functions in activities, it is time to look at the structure of Jetpack Compose-based projects. While Android Studio sets everything up for you if you create a Compose app using the project wizard, it is important to know which files are involved under the hood.

Looking under the hood

Jetpack Compose heavily relies on Kotlin. This means that your app project must be configured to use Kotlin. It does not imply, though, that you cannot use Java at all. In fact, you can easily mix Kotlin and Java in your project, as long as your composable functions are written in Kotlin. You can also combine traditional views and composables. I will be discussing this topic in *Chapter 9, Exploring Interoperability APIs*.

First, make sure to configure the Android Gradle plugin that corresponds to your version of Android Studio in the project-level build.gradle file:

```
buildscript {
  ...
  dependencies {
    classpath "com.android.tools.build:gradle:7.0.4"
    classpath "org.jetbrains.kotlin:kotlin-gradle-
              plugin:1.5.31"
    ...
  }
}
```

The following code snippets belong in the module-level build.gradle file:

```
plugins {
    id 'com.android.application'
    id 'kotlin-android'
}
```

Next, please make sure that your app's minimum API level is set to 21 or higher and that Jetpack Compose is enabled. The following code snippet also sets the version for the Kotlin compiler plugin:

```
android {
  defaultConfig {
    ...
    minSdkVersion 21
  }
  buildFeatures {
    compose true
  }
  ...
  compileOptions {
    sourceCompatibility JavaVersion.VERSION_11
    targetCompatibility JavaVersion.VERSION_11
  }
  kotlinOptions {
    jvmTarget = "11"
```

```
    }
composeOptions {
    kotlinCompilerExtensionVersion compose_version
    }
}
```

Finally, declare dependencies. The following code snippet acts as a good starting point. Depending on which packages your app uses, you may need additional ones:

```
dependencies {
    implementation 'androidx.core:core-ktx:1.7.0'
    implementation 'androidx.appcompat:appcompat:1.4.0'
    Implementation
        "androidx.compose.ui:ui:$compose_version"
    implementation
        "androidx.compose.material:material:$compose_version"
    implementation
        "androidx.compose.ui:ui-tooling-
        preview:$compose_version"
    implementation
        'androidx.lifecycle:lifecycle-runtime-ktx:2.4.0'
    implementation
        'androidx.activity:activity-compose:1.4.0'
    debugImplementation
        "androidx.compose.ui:ui-tooling:$compose_version"
}
```

Once you have configured your project, building and running a Compose app works just like traditional view-based apps.

Pressing the play button

To run your Compose app, select your target device, make sure that the **app** module is selected, and press the green *play* button (*Figure 1.8*):

Figure 1.8 – Android Studio toolbar elements to launch an app

Congratulations! Well done. You have now launched your first Compose app, and you have achieved quite a lot. Let's recap.

Summary

In this chapter, we learned how to write our first composables: Kotlin functions that have been annotated with @Composable. Composable functions are the core building blocks of Jetpack Compose-based UIs. You combined existing library composables with your own to create beautiful app screens. To see a preview, we can add the @Preview annotation. To use Jetpack Compose in a project, both build.gradle files must be configured accordingly.

In *Chapter 2, Understanding the Declarative Paradigm*, we will take a closer look at the differences between the declarative approach of Jetpack Compose and the imperative nature of traditional UI frameworks such as Android's view-based component library.

Further reading

This book assumes you have a basic understanding of the syntax of Kotlin and Android development in general. If you would like to learn more about this, I suggest looking at *Android Programming with Kotlin for Beginners, John Horton, Packt Publishing, 2019, ISBN 9781789615401.*

2
Understanding the Declarative Paradigm

Jetpack Compose marks a fundamental shift in Android UI development. While the traditional view-based approach is centered around components and classes, the new framework follows a declarative approach.

In *Chapter 1, Building Your First Compose App*, I introduced you to composable functions, the basic building blocks of a Compose-based UI. In this chapter, we will briefly review how Android UIs are implemented with traditional classes and techniques. You will learn about some issues of this approach, and how a declarative framework helps overcome them.

The main sections of this chapter are as follows:

- Looking at the Android view system
- Moving from components to composable functions
- Examining architectural concepts

We'll start by looking at my second sample app, *Hello View*. It is a re-implementation of the *Hello* app from *Chapter 1, Building Your First Compose App*. *Hello View* uses views, an XML **layout file**, and **view binding**.

Next, we will cover key aspects of **components**, which are UI building blocks in the view-based world. You will learn about the similarities and differences of composable functions, and we will find out how composable functions can overcome some of the limitations of component-centric frameworks.

Finally, we will look at the different layers of the Android framework and how they relate to building UIs. By the end of this chapter, you will have gathered enough background information to explore the key principles of Jetpack Compose, which is the topic of the next chapter.

Technical requirements

Please refer to the *Technical requirements* section in *Chapter 1, Building Your First Compose App*, for information about how to install and set up Android Studio and how to get the sample app. All the code files for this chapter can be found on GitHub at https://github.com/PacktPublishing/Android-UI-Development-with-Jetpack-Compose/tree/main/chapter_02.

Looking at the Android view system

The traditional approach to building Android UIs is to define component trees and modify them during runtime. While this can be done completely programmatically, the preferred way is to create layout files. They use XML tags and attributes to define which UI elements should be presented on screen. Let's take a look:

```xml
<?xml version="1.0" encoding="utf-8"?>
<androidx.constraintlayout.widget.ConstraintLayout
  xmlns:android="http://schemas.android.com/apk/res/android"
  xmlns:app="http://schemas.android.com/apk/res-auto"
  android:layout_width="match_parent"
  android:layout_height="match_parent">

  <TextView
    android:id="@+id/message"
    style="@style/TextAppearance.AppCompat.Medium"
    android:layout_width="wrap_content"
```

```
    android:layout_height="wrap_content"
    android:textAlignment="center"
    app:layout_constraintBottom_toBottomOf="parent"
    app:layout_constraintBottom_toTopOf="@id/name"
    app:layout_constraintEnd_toEndOf="parent"
    app:layout_constraintHorizontal_bias="0.5"
    app:layout_constraintStart_toStartOf="parent"
    app:layout_constraintTop_toTopOf="parent"
    app:layout_constraintVertical_bias="0.5"
    app:layout_constraintVertical_chainStyle="packed" />
    ...
</androidx.constraintlayout.widget.ConstraintLayout>
```

Layout files define a hierarchical structure (a tree). In the previous XML snippet, the root node (ConstraintLayout) contains only one child (TextView). The complete XML file of *Hello View* has two more children, an EditText component and a Button component. Layout files of real-world apps can be quite nested, containing dozens of children.

Generally speaking, . . . Layout elements are responsible for sizing and positioning their children. While they may have a visual representation (for example, background color or a border), they usually don't interact with the user. ScrollView is one of the exceptions to that rule. All other (non . . . Layout) elements such as buttons, checkboxes, and editable text fields not only allow for user interaction – it's their purpose.

Both layout and non-layout elements are called components. We will return to this term in the *Moving from components to composable functions* section. But before that, let's see how layout files are used in apps.

Inflating layout files

Activities are one of the core building blocks of an Android app. They implement a quite sophisticated lifecycle, which is reflected by a couple of methods we can override.

Typically, onCreate() is used to prepare the app and to show the UI by invoking setContentView(). This method can receive an ID representing a layout file, for example, R.layout.main. Because of this, you must define variables pointing to the UI elements you wish to access. This may look like the following:

```
private lateinit var doneButton: Button
...
val doneButton = findViewById(R.id.done)
```

It turned out that this doesn't scale well for bigger apps. There are two important issues to remember:

- You may face crashes during runtime if the variable is accessed before it has been initialized.

- The code quickly becomes lengthy if you have more than a few components.

Sometimes, you can prevent the first issue by using local variables, as follows:

```
val doneButton = findViewById<Button>(R.id.done)
```

This way, you can access the UI element immediately after the declaration. But the variable exists only in the scope in which it has been defined – a block or a function. This may be problematic because you often need to modify a component outside onCreate(). That's because in a component-based world, you modify the UI by modifying the properties of a component. It turned out that often the same set of changes are necessary for different parts of the app, so to avoid code duplication, they are refactored into methods, which need to know the component to change it.

To solve the second issue – that is, to spare the developer from the task of keeping references to components – Google introduced view binding. It belongs to Jetpack and debuted in Android Studio 3.6. Let's see how it is used:

```
class MainActivity : AppCompatActivity() {

    private lateinit var binding: MainBinding

    override fun onCreate(savedInstanceState: Bundle?) {
        super.onCreate(savedInstanceState)
        binding = MainBinding.inflate(layoutInflater)
        setContentView(binding.root)
        ...
        enableOrDisableButton()
    }
    ...
}
```

No matter how complex the UI of an activity is, we need to keep only one reference. This variable is usually called `binding`, which is initialized by invoking `inflate()` of a `...Binding` instance. The `MainBinding` class in my example is automatically generated and updated, when `main.xml` is modified. Every layout file gets a corresponding `...Binding` class. To enable this mechanism, the `viewBinding` build option must be set to `true` in the module-level `build.gradle` file:

```
android {
  ...
  buildFeatures {
    viewBinding true
  }
}
```

So, after you have inflated a layout file by invoking `...Binding.inflate()` and assigned it to an instance variable, you can access all of its components via their IDs using this variable. IDs are set using the XML attribute `android:id` (for example, `android:id="@+id/message"`).

> **Important Note**
> There is an important difference between the old-fashioned `findViewById()` and view binding. If you use the latter one, you must pass the root component (`binding.root`) to `setContentView()`, rather than an ID representing the layout file (`R.layout.main`).

In this section, I have shown you how to obtain references to UI elements. The next section, *Modifying the UI*, will explain how to make use of this.

Modifying the UI

In this section, we will see how to make changes to a View-based UI. Let's start by looking at the `enableOrDisableButton()` function, which is invoked in `onCreate()`. Its name gives you a clue regarding its purpose – enabling or disabling a button. But why do we need this? *Hello View* is a reimplementation of the *Hello* app from *Chapter 1, Building Your First Compose App*, but it has one additional feature. As long as the user has not entered at least one non-blank character, **Done** can't be clicked:

```
private fun enableOrDisableButton() {
  binding.done.isEnabled = binding.name.text.isNotBlank()
}
```

`binding.done` refers to the button during runtime. It can be clicked only if
`isEnabled` is `true`. The text input field is denoted by `binding.name`. Its `text`
property reflects what the user has already entered. `isNotBlank()` tells us if at least one
non-whitespace character is present.

In the code I have shown you so far, `enableOrDisableButton()` is called only at
the end of `onCreate()`. But we also need to invoke the function whenever the user has
input something. Let's see how to do this (please note that the following code snippets
belong inside `onCreate()` so that they are executed when the activity is created):

```
binding.name.run {
    setOnEditorActionListener { _, _, _ ->
        binding.done.performClick()
        true
    }
    doAfterTextChanged {
        enableOrDisableButton()
    }
    visibility = VISIBLE
}
```

Text input fields can modify certain aspects of the onscreen keyboard. For
example, to have it show a **Done** key instead of the usual **Enter**, we add an
`android:imeOptions="actionDone"` attribute to the layout file. To react to clicks
on this key, we need to register code by invoking `setOnEditorActionListener()`.
Then, `binding.done.performClick()` simulates clicks on the **Done** button.
You will see shortly why I do this.

The lambda function we pass to `doAfterTextChanged()` is invoked every time
the user enters or deletes something in the text input field. When this happens,
`enableOrDisableButton()` is called, which makes the button clickable if the text
currently present in the input field is not blank.

Finally, `visibility = VISIBLE` occurs inside `binding.name.run {`, so it makes
the text input field visible. This is the desired state when the activity is created.

Now, let's turn to code related to the **Done** button:

```
binding.done.run {
    setOnClickListener {
        val name = binding.name.text
        if (name.isNotBlank()) {
```

```
        binding.message.text = getString(R.string.hello,
                                        name)
        binding.name.visibility = GONE
        it.visibility = GONE
    }
}
visibility = VISIBLE
}
```

When **Done** is clicked, we test whether the text input field contains at least one character besides whitespace. If this is the case, the greeting message will be constructed and displayed. Also, both the button and the text input field are hidden; they need to disappear after the user has entered a name, because then only the greeting message should be visible. Making a component visible or invisible is done by modifying the `visibility` property: `visibility = VISIBLE` makes the **Done** button visible. This is the desired state when the activity is created.

Do you remember that I promised to explain why I invoke `performClick()` inside the lambda function for `setOnEditorActionListener`? This way, I can reuse the code inside the button listener without refactoring it into a separate function and calling it instead, which certainly is a viable alternative.

Before we move on, let's recap what have we seen so far:

- The UI is defined in an XML file.
- At runtime, it is inflated to a component tree.
- To change the UI, attributes of all related components must be modified.
- Even if a UI element is not visible, it remains part of the component tree.

This is why common UI frameworks are called **imperative**. Any change to the UI is done by deliberately modifying the attributes of all components involved. As you can see in my example, this works quite well for small apps. But the more UI elements an app has, the more demanding it will be to keep track of such changes. Let me explain. Changes in domain data (adding an item to a list, deleting text, or loading an image from a remote service) require changes in the UI. The developer needs to know which portion of domain data relates to which UI element and must then modify the component tree accordingly. The bigger an app becomes, the more difficult this is.

Also, without clear architectural guidance, the code for changing the component tree almost always eventually mixes with code that modifies data the app is using. This makes it even more demanding and error-prone to maintain and further develop the app. In the next section, we will turn to composable functions. You will learn how they differ from components and why this helps overcome weaknesses in the imperative approach.

Moving from components to composable functions

So far, I explained the word *component* by saying that it refers to UI elements. In fact, the term is used in quite a few other areas. Generally speaking, components structure systems by separating distinct portions or parts of them. The inner workings of a component are typically hidden from the outside (known as the **black box principle**).

> **Tip**
> To learn more about the black box principle, please refer to `https://en.wikipedia.org/wiki/Black_box`.

Components communicate with other parts of the system by sending and receiving messages. The appearance or behavior of a component is controlled through a set of attributes, or **properties**.

Consider `TextView`. We set text by modifying the `text` property and we control its visibility through `visibility`. What about sending and receiving messages? Let's look at `Button`. We can react to clicks (receive a message) by registering (sending a message) an `OnClickListener` instance. The same principle applies to `EditText`. We configure its appearance through setting properties (`text`), send a message by invoking `setOnEditorActionListener()`, and receive one through the lambda expression we passed as a parameter.

Message-based communication and configuration via properties make components very tool-friendly. In fact, most component-based UI frameworks work well with drawing board-like editors. The developer defines a UI using drag and drop. Components are configured using property sheets. *Figure 2.1* shows the Layout Editor in Android Studio. You can switch between a **Design** view, browse **Code** (an XML file), or a combination of both (**Split**):

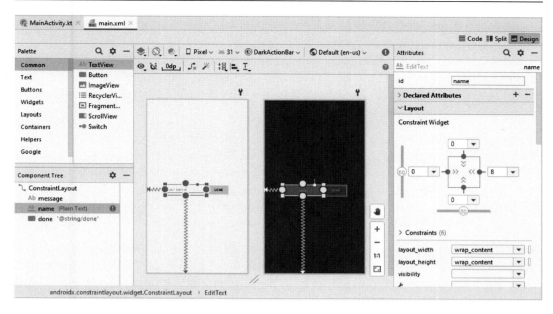

Figure 2.1 – The Layout Editor in Android Studio

We now have a more precise understanding of how the *component* term is used in the context of UIs. Building on this foundation, we will now look at component hierarchies.

Component hierarchies

If you compare the XML attributes of `ConstraintLayout`, `TextView`, and `EditText`, you will find unique attributes per tag, one example being `android:inputType`. On the other hand, `android:layout_width` and `android:layout_height` are present in all three tags, defining the size of the corresponding element. Size and position are relevant for all components.

Yet, specific attributes influence visual appearance or behavior; this is *not* relevant for all kinds of UI elements, only a subset. Here's an example: text fields and buttons will want to show or receive text. A `FrameLayout` UI element won't. Think of it this way: the *more specialized* an attribute is, the *less likely is its reuse* in another component. However, general ones (such as `width`, `height`, `location`, or `color`) will be needed in most UI elements.

Based on its attributes, each component has a level of specialization. For example, `EditText` is more specific than `TextView` because it can handle text input. `Button` is a general-purpose button; clicking on it triggers some action. On the other hand, a `CheckBox` component can be either checked or unchecked. This type of button can represent two states. A `Switch` component has two states, too. It's a toggle switch widget that can select between two options.

The degree of specialization can be modeled easily in object-oriented programming languages through inheritance. A more specialized UI element (class) extends a general element. Therefore, many often-used UI frameworks have been implemented in Java, C++, or C# (object-oriented languages). It is important to note, though, that component-like concepts can be achieved with other types of programming languages too. So, object orientation may be considered a benefit, but it's not a necessity.

At this point, you may be thinking, *Didn't he mix two different things? How are tags and attributes of Android layout files related to classes?* Allow me to explain. Earlier, I said that an XML file is **inflated** to a component tree. To be more precise – it becomes an *object* tree. The tags in the XML file represent class names and its attributes correspond to members of that class. `inflate()` creates a tree of objects based on this information.

So, Android layout files describe component trees outside of Java or Kotlin files using a different syntax (an XML syntax). But they are not declarative in the same way Jetpack Compose is because layout files define a UI regardless of the current state. For example, they do not take into account that a button should be disabled because a text field is empty. A Compose UI, on the other hand, is declared *based* on that.

The remaining part of this section will look closer at some of Android's UI components and how they are related. Before that, let's recap what we have learned so far:

- All Android views are classes.
- Tags in layout files represent classes and attributes are their members.
- `inflate()` creates an object tree.
- Changes to the UI are achieved by modifying this tree.

Some of Android's UI elements are quite specific. `RatingBar`, for example, allows the user to rate something by selecting a certain number of stars. Others are way more general; for example, `ImageView` just displays image resources, and `FrameLayout` blocks out an area on the screen to display a stack of children.

To understand how Android's UI elements are related, let's look at the ones used in *Hello View* in a little more detail. We'll start with `ConstraintLayout`:

```
java.lang.Object
  ↳ android.view.View
    ↳ android.view.ViewGroup
      ↳ androidx.constraintlayout.widget.ConstraintLayout
```

The root of *all* classes in Java is `java.lang.Object`. Significant parts of the Android framework are based on Java and its class library. So, all views directly or indirectly extend `java.lang.Object`. The immediate parent of `ConstraintLayout` is `android.view.ViewGroup`, which in turn is a sibling of `android.view.View`.

Now, let's look at `android.widget.Button`.

```
java.lang.Object
  ↳ android.view.View
    ↳ android.widget.TextView
      ↳ android.widget.Button
```

Its direct ancestor is `android.widget.TextView`, which extends `android.view.View`. Are we seeing a pattern here? `android.view.View` seems to be the root of all Android UI elements. Let's check our hypothesis by examining another component:

```
java.lang.Object
  ↳ android.view.View
    ↳ android.widget.TextView
      ↳ android.widget.EditText
```

As you can see, components showing or receiving text usually extend `android.widget.TextView`, whose parent is `android.view.View`.

> **Important Note**
> `android.view.View` is the root of all Android UI elements. All components that position and size their children extend `android.view.ViewGroup`.

So far, structuring UI elements in a hierarchy based on specialization seems to work well. Unfortunately, this approach does have limitations. We'll turn to them in the following section.

Limitations of component hierarchies

Buttons usually show text. Therefore, it seems natural to extend a more general text component. As we have seen in the previous section, Android does just that. What if your app requires a button that has no text and shows an image instead? In such scenarios, you can use ImageButton:

```
java.lang.Object
 ↳  android.view.View
     ↳  android.widget.ImageView
         ↳  android.widget.ImageButton
```

The class extends android.widget.ImageView. This makes sense, as the purpose of this component is to show just an image, quite like Button and text. But what if we want to show a button that contains both text and image? The closest common ancestor of ImageButton and an ordinary text button is android.view.View, the root of the Android UI element hierarchy. Therefore, everything Button inherits from TextView is not immediately available to ImageButton (and vice versa).

The reason is that Java is based upon **single inheritance**: a class extends exactly one other class. If Button wanted to take advantage of the features of TextView and ImageView, it would need to extend both, which it can't. Does this mean that things would be different if Java supported **multiple inheritance**? We could combine the behavior of several components, but we still wouldn't be able to reuse functionality tied to *individual* attributes, methods, or sets of them. Let's see why this is important.

The View class knows about padding (providing space to the inside of its bounds) but not about margins (space to the outside of its bounds). Margins are defined in ViewGroup. Hence, if a component wants to use them, it must extend ViewGroup. But in doing so, it inevitably inherits all other features of this class (for example, the ability to layout children), regardless of needing them or not. The underlying issue is that in a component-centric framework, the combination of *individual features* of one or more components to create a more specialized UI element is not possible because you cannot cut out these features. The reason for this is that reuse happens at a component level.

To make individual features reusable, we need to put aside the notion of components. That's what, for example, Flutter (the very successful cross-platform alternative to Jetpack Compose) does. Its UI framework is fully declarative, still class-based. Flutter relies on a simple principle called **composition over inheritance**. It means the look and the behavior of a UI element (and the complete UI) are defined by combining simple building blocks, such as Container, Padding, Align, or GestureDetector, rather than modifying a parent.

In Jetpack Compose, we combine simple building blocks too. Instead of classes, we use composable functions. Before we turn to them, I would like to briefly show you another potential issue of components.

As you have seen, in class-based UI component frameworks, specialization is modeled through inheritance. The specialized version of a class (which may have new features, a new look, or behave slightly different than the ancestor) extends a more general version of the class. However, most object-oriented programming languages provide means to prohibit this; for example, if a Java class is marked final or a Kotlin class is not open, they cannot be extended.

So, the framework developer can make a deliberate decision to prevent further inheritance. `android.widget.Space`, a lightweight `View` subclass to create gaps between UI elements, is final. The same applies to `android.view.ViewStub`. It's an invisible, zero-sized `View` used to lazily inflate layout resources at runtime. Fortunately, most of Android's UI elements can be extended. And for both examples, it seems unlikely that we would want to extend them. Hence, you may not face this potential issue at all. The point is that in a framework based upon composition rather than inheritance, it doesn't matter.

Composing UIs with functions

Now it's time to return to composable functions. In this section, we will look at my sample app *Factorial* (*Figure 2.2*). When the user picks a number between 0 and 9, its factorial (the product of it and all the integers below it greater than 0) is computed and output, like so:

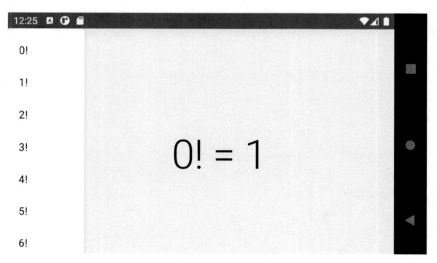

Figure 2.2 – The Factorial app

Here is the simple function that creates the output text:

```kotlin
fun factorialAsString(n: Int): String {
  var result = 1L
  for (i in 1..n) {
    result *= i
  }
  return "$n! = $result"
}
```

The factorial of an n non-negative integer value is the product of all positive integers less than or equal to n. So, the result can be computed easily by multiplying all integers between 1 and n. Please note that the maximum value of a Kotlin Long type is 9,223,372,036,854,775,807. Hence, my implementation does not work if result would need to be bigger than that.

Next, I'll show you how the UI is composed:

```kotlin
@Composable
fun Factorial() {
  var expanded by remember { mutableStateOf(false) }
  var text by remember {
    mutableStateOf(factorialAsString(0)) }
  Box(
    modifier = Modifier.fillMaxSize(),
    contentAlignment = Alignment.Center
  ) {
    Text(
      modifier = Modifier.clickable {
        expanded = true
      },
      text = text,
      style = MaterialTheme.typography.h2
    )
    DropdownMenu(
      expanded = expanded,
      onDismissRequest = {
        expanded = false
      }) {
```

```
for (n in 0 until 10) {
  DropdownMenuItem(onClick = {
    expanded = false
    text = factorialAsString(n)
  }) {
    Text("${n.toString()}!")
  }
}
```

The `Factorial()` composable function contains one predefined composable, `Box()`, which in turn has two children, `Text()` and `DropdownMenu()`. I briefly introduced you to `Text()` and `Box()` in *Chapter 1, Building Your First Compose App*. So let's concentrate on `DropdownMenu()`.

A drop-down menu (the equivalent to a `Spinner`) displays a list of entries in a compact way. It appears upon interaction with an element, such as the following:

- An icon or a button
- When the user performs a specific action

In my example, the `Text()` composable must be clicked.

The content of a menu can either be provided by a `for` loop statement or by adding it one by one. Often, but not necessarily, `DropdownMenuItem()` is used. If the menu is expanded (that is, open or visible), it is controlled by the `expanded` parameter. `onDismissRequest` is used to react to closing the menu without selecting something. `DropdownMenuItem()` receives a click handler via the `onClick` parameter. That code is executed when the item is clicked.

So far, I have presented quite a lot of information about composable functions to you. Before we move on, let's recap what we know so far:

- The entry point of a Compose UI is a composable function.
- From there, other composable functions are called.
- Often, composable functions receive *content* that is other composables.
- The order of invocation controls where a UI element will be in relation to other UI elements.

Let's continue with how `Factorial()` works. It defines two variables, `expanded` and `text`. But how are they used? While an Android layout file defines a component tree in its initial state, a composable UI is always declared using actual data. This means that there is no need to set up or prepare the UI before it can be displayed for the first time. Whenever it is displayed, it looks the way you want. Let's see how this works.

Most composable functions are configured by a set of parameters. Some of them are mandatory; others can be omitted. The important thing is that the composable is always called with actual values. On the other hand, components (that is, views) are initialized when they are created. And they remain this way until they are deliberately changed by altering the value of properties. That's why an app needs to keep references to all components (UI elements) it wishes to modify. But how is a Compose UI updated?

The process of updating a Compose UI is called **recomposition**. It takes place automatically whenever a composable function being part of the UI needs to be updated. This is the case when some of the values that influence its look or behavior (parameters) change. If you always pass the same text to `Text()`, there is no need to recompose it. If, on the other hand, you pass something Jetpack Compose knows it can change, the Compose runtime will initiate an update, a recomposition, when that change happens. Values that change over time are called **state**. You can create state, for example, using `mutableStateOf()`. To refer to state in a composable, you need to `remember` it in that composable function.

Both `expanded` and `text` contain state. When these variables are used as parameters for composable functions, those composables will be recomposed whenever the value of these variables changes. Setting `expanded` to `true` brings the drop-down menu on screen immediately. This is done inside a lambda function passed to `clickable {}`. I will be discussing this in the next section. Giving `text` a new value changes the display of `Text()` because we pass the variable `text` as the value of the equally named parameter. This happens, for example, inside the code block passed to `onClick`.

Getting rid of a component tree (that needs to be updated deliberately) in favor of declaring a UI based on state and thus getting updates upon state changes for free is possibly one of the most exciting advantages of the declarative approach. In the next section, I will explain a few more architectural principles of component-based and declarative UI frameworks.

Examining architectural aspects

In the *Component hierarchies* section, I showed you that component-based UI frameworks rely on specialization. General features and concepts are implemented in the root component or one of its immediate successors. Such general features include the following:

- Location and size on screen
- Basic visual aspects like background (color)
- Simple user interactions (reacting to clicks)

Any component will provide these features, either in a specialized way or in its basic implementation. Android's view system is class-based, so changing functionality is done by overriding the methods of the parent.

Composable functions, on the other hand, do not have a shared set of properties. By annotating a function with @Composable, we make certain parts of Jetpack Compose aware of it. But besides not specifying a return type, composables seem to have few things in common. However, this would have been a pretty short-sighted architectural decision. In fact, Jetpack Compose makes providing a simple, predictable API really easy. The remaining part of this section illustrates this by showing you how to react to clicks, and how to size and position UI elements.

Reacting to clicks

Android's View class contains a method called setOnClickListener(). It receives a View.OnClickListener instance. This interface contains one method, onClick(View v). The implementation of this method provides the code that should be executed when the view is clicked. Additionally, there is a view property called clickable. It is accessed through setClickable() and isClickable(). If clickable is set to false after the listener has been set, the click event will not be delivered (onClick() is not called).

Jetpack Compose can provide click handling in two ways. Firstly, composable functions that require it (because it is a core feature for them) have a dedicated onClick parameter. Secondly, composables that usually do not require click handling can be amended with a modifier. Let's start with the first one.

```
@Composable
@Preview
fun ButtonDemo() {
  Box {
    Button(onClick = {
```

```
        println("clicked")
    }) {
      Text("Click me!")
    }
  }
}
```

Please note that onClick is mandatory; you must provide it.

If you want to show the button but the user should not be able to click it, the code looks like this:

```
Button(
  onClick = {
    println("clicked")
  },
  enabled = false
) {
  Text("Click me!")
}
```

Figure 2.3 shows what the button looks like when enabled is either true or false:

Figure 2.3 – A button with enabled = true or false

Text() doesn't have an onClick property. If you want to make it clickable (like I do in the *Factorial* app), you pass clickable { ... } to the modifier parameter:

```
modifier = Modifier.clickable { ...
```

Modifiers, as their name suggests, provide an infrastructure for influencing both the visual appearance and behavior of composable functions. I will show you another example for modifiers in the next section. *Chapter 3, Exploring the Key Principles of Compose*, covers them in much greater detail.

Sizing and positioning UI elements

In component-centric UI frameworks, size and location onscreen (or relative to another component) are core properties. They are defined in the root component (on Android, the `View` class). Descendants of `ViewGroup` size and position their children by changing their corresponding properties. For example, `RelativeLayout` is based upon instructions such as `toStartOf`, `toEndOf`, or `below`. `FrameLayout` draws its children in a stack. And `LinearLayout` lays out children horizontally or vertically. So, `...Layout`s are containers with the ability to size and position their children.

Jetpack Compose has a very similar concept. You have already learned about `Row()` and `Column()`, which lay out their content horizontally or vertically. `Box()` is similar to `FrameLayout`. It organizes its content in the order it appears in code. The position inside the box is controlled by `contentAlignment`:

```
@Composable
@Preview
fun BoxDemo() {
  Box(contentAlignment = Alignment.Center) {
    Box(
        modifier = Modifier
          .size(width = 100.dp, height = 100.dp)
          .background(Color.Green)
    )
    Box(
        modifier = Modifier
          .size(width = 80.dp, height = 80.dp)
          .background(Color.Yellow)
    )
    Text(
        text = "Hello",
        color = Color.Black,
        modifier = Modifier.align(Alignment.TopStart)
    )
  }
}
```

The content may override this by using `modifier = Modifier.align()`, the result of which we can see in *Figure 2.4*:

Figure 2.4 – An invisible box containing two colored boxes and text

Modifiers can also be used to request a size. In some of my examples, you may have spotted `Modifier.fillMaxSize()`, which makes the composable as big as possible. `Modifier.size()` requests a particular size. Modifiers can be chained. The root of such a chain is the `Modifier` companion object. Subsequent modifiers are added using a dot.

Before closing this chapter, I would like to emphasize the benefits of the modifier concept with one more example. Did you notice the `background()` modifiers of the first and second content box? This modifier allows you to set a background color for any composable function. When you need something a composable function does not offer out of the box, you can add it with a modifier. As you can write custom modifiers, the possibilities to adjust a composable to your needs are almost endless. I will elaborate on this in the next chapter.

Summary

In this chapter, you have learned about key elements of component-centric UI frameworks. We saw some of the limitations of this approach and how the declarative paradigm can overcome them. For example, specialization takes place on a component level. If the framework is based upon inheritance, the distribution of features to children may be too broad. Jetpack Compose tackles this with the modifier mechanism, which allows us to amend functionality at a very fine-grained level; this means that composables only get the functionality they need (for example, a background color).

The remaining chapters of this book are solely based on the declarative approach. In *Chapter 3, Exploring the Key Principles of Compose*, we will take an even closer look at composable functions and examine the concepts of composition and recomposition. And, as promised, we will also dive deep into modifiers.

3

Exploring the Key Principles of Compose

In the first chapter of this book, we built and run our first Jetpack Compose app. Then, in *Chapter 2, Understanding the Declarative Paradigm*, we explained the imperative nature of Android's traditional UI toolkit, illustrated some of its weaknesses, and saw how a declarative approach can overcome them.

In this chapter, we build upon these foundations by examining a few key principles Jetpack Compose relies on. This knowledge is essential for writing well-behaving Compose apps. This chapter introduces these key principles.

In this chapter, we will cover the following topics:

- Looking closer at composable functions
- Composing and recomposing the **user interface** (**UI**)
- Modifying the behavior of composable functions

We will start by revisiting composable functions, the building blocks of a composable UI. This time, we will dig much deeper into their underlying ideas and concepts. By the end of the first main section, you will have established a thorough understanding of what composable functions are, how they are written, and how they are used.

The following section focuses on creating and updating the UI. You will learn how Jetpack Compose achieves what other UI frameworks call repainting. This mechanism, which is called **recomposition** in Compose, takes place automatically whenever something relevant to the UI changes. To keep this process fluent, your composable functions must adhere to a few best practices. I will explain them to you in this section.

We will close this chapter by expanding our knowledge of the concept of modifiers. We will take a close look at how modifier chains work and what you need to keep in mind to always get the intended results. You will also learn how to implement custom modifiers. They allow you to amend any composable function to look or behave in precisely the way you want them to.

Now, let's get started!

Technical requirements

Please refer to the *Technical requirements* section of *Chapter 1, Building Your First Compose App*, for information on how to install and set up Android Studio, as well as how to get the sample apps. If you want to try the `ShortColoredTextDemo()` and `ColoredTextDemo()` composables from the *Looking closer at composable functions* section, you can use the `Sandbox` app project in the top-level directory of this book's GitHub repository at `https://github.com/PacktPublishing/Android-UI-Development-with-Jetpack-Compose`. Open `SandboxActivity` and copy the composable functions from `code_snippets.txt`, which will be located in the `/chapter_03` folder.

Looking closer at composable functions

The UI of a Compose app is built by writing and calling composable functions. We have already done both in the previous chapters, but my explanations regarding the structure of a composable, as well as its internals, have been quite basic – it's time to fix that.

Building blocks of composable functions

A **composable function** is a Kotlin function that has been annotated with `@Composable`. All composables *must* be marked this way because the annotation informs the Compose compiler that the function converts data into UI elements.

The signature of a Kotlin function consists of the following parts or building blocks:

- An optional visibility modifier (`private`, `protected`, `internal`, or `public`)
- The `fun` keyword
- A name
- A list of parameters (can be empty) or, optionally, a default value
- An optional return type
- A block of code

Let's explore these parts in greater detail.

The default visibility (if you omit the modifier) is `public`. This means that the (composable) function can be called from anywhere. If a function is meant to be reused (for example, a text styled to match your brand), it should be publicly available. On the other hand, if a function is tied to a particular **context** (the region of code, such as a class), it may make sense to restrict its access. There is an open debate on how rigid the visibility of functions should be restrained. In the end, you and your team need to agree on a point of view and stick to it. For the sake of simplicity, my examples are usually public.

The name of a composable function uses the *PascalCase* notation: it starts with an uppercase letter, whereas the remaining characters are lowercase. If the name consists of more than one word, each word follows this rule. The name should be a noun (`Demo`), or a noun that has been prefixed with a descriptive adjective (`FancyDemo`). Unlike other (ordinary) Kotlin functions, it should *not* be a verb or a verb phrase (`getDataFromServer`). The *API Guidelines for Jetpack Compose* file, which is available at `https://github.com/androidx/androidx/blob/androidx-main/compose/docs/compose-api-guidelines.md`, details these naming conventions.

All the data you want to pass to a composable function is provided through a comma-separated list, which is enclosed in parenthesis. If a composable does not require values, the list remains empty. Here's a composable function that can receive two parameters:

```
@Composable
fun ColoredTextDemo(
    text: String = "",
```

```
    color: Color = Color.Black
) {
    Text(
        text = text,
        style = TextStyle(color = color)
    )
}
```

In Kotlin, function parameters are defined as `name: type`. Parameters are separated by a comma. You can specify a default value by adding `= ....` This is used if no value is provided for a particular parameter when the function is being invoked.

The return type of a function is optional. In this case, the function returns `Unit`. `Unit` is a type with only one value: `Unit`. If, like in this example, it is omitted, the function body follows immediately after the list of arguments. Most composable functions you will be writing do not need to return anything, so do not need a return type. Situations that require it will be covered in the *Returning values* section.

If the code of a function contains more than one statement or expression, it will be enclosed in curly braces. Kotlin offers a nice abbreviation for if just one expression needs to be executed – Jetpack Compose itself uses this quite frequently.

```
@Composable
fun ShortColoredTextDemo(
    text: String = "",
    color: Color = Color.Black
) = Text(
    text = text,
    style = TextStyle(color = color)
)
```

As you can see, the expression follows an equals sign. This means that `ShortColoredTextDemo()` returns whatever `Text()` is returning.

Unlike Java, Kotlin does not know about the `void` keyword, so all the functions must return *something*. By omitting the return type, we implicitly tell Kotlin that the return type of a function is `kotlin.Unit`. This type has only one value: the `Unit` object. So, `Unit` corresponds to `void` in Java.

Let's test this by printing the result of invoking a composable function:

```kotlin
class SandboxActivity : ComponentActivity() {
    override fun onCreate(savedInstanceState: Bundle?) {
        super.onCreate(savedInstanceState)
        setContent {
            println(ColoredTextDemo(
                text = "Hello Compose",
                color = Color.Blue
            ))
        }
    }
}
```

If you run the app, the following line will be printed:

```
I/System.out: kotlin.Unit
```

While this may not look too exciting, its implications are profound. Think of it: although the `ColoredTextDemo()` composable function returns nothing interesting, some text is shown on the screen. This happens because it invokes another composable, called `Text()`. So, whatever may be needed to show text must happen inside `Text()`, and it cannot have anything to do with the return value of a composable.

In the previous chapter, I said that composable functions *emit* UI elements. I will explain what this means in the next section.

Emitting UI elements

A Compose UI is created by nesting calls to composable functions, which can be provided by the Jetpack Compose libraries, code of other developers, or your app.

Let's find out what happens once `ColoredTextDemo()` has called `androidx.compose.material.Text()`. To see the source code of (among others) composable functions in Android Studio, you can click on their names while holding down the *Ctrl* key (on a Mac, it's the *cmd* key).

> **Please Note**
>
> I will only show you the important steps because otherwise, I would need to copy too much code. To get the best learning experience, please follow the call chain directly in your IDE.

`Text()` defines two variables, `textColor` and `mergedStyle`, and passes them to `androidx.compose.foundation.text.BasicText()`. Although you can use `BasicText()` in your code, you should choose `androidx.compose.material.Text()` if possible, because it consumes style information from a theme. Please refer to *Chapter 6, Putting Pieces Together*, for more information about themes.

`BasicText()` immediately delegates to `CoreText()`, which belongs to the `androidx.compose.foundation.text` package too. It is an internal composable function, meaning you can't use it in your apps.

`CoreText()` initializes and remembers quite a few variables. There is no need to explain them all here, but the most important piece is the invocation of another composable function: `Layout()`.

`Layout()` belongs to the `androidx.compose.ui.layout` package. It is the core composable function for the layout, with its purpose being to size and position children. *Chapter 4, Laying Out UI Elements*, covers this in great detail. Right now, we still need to find out what *emitting UI elements* means. So, let's see what `Layout()` does:

```
66   @Suppress( …names: "ComposableLambdaParameterPosition")
67   @Composable inline fun Layout(
68       content: @Composable () -> Unit,
69       modifier: Modifier = Modifier,
70       measurePolicy: MeasurePolicy
71   ) {
72       val density = LocalDensity.current
73       val layoutDirection = LocalLayoutDirection.current
74       ReusableComposeNode<ComposeUiNode, Applier<Any>>(
75           factory = ComposeUiNode.Constructor,
76           update = {  this: Updater<ComposeUiNode>
77               set(measurePolicy, ComposeUiNode.SetMeasurePolicy)
78               set(density, ComposeUiNode.SetDensity)
79               set(layoutDirection, ComposeUiNode.SetLayoutDirection)
80           },
81           skippableUpdate = materializerOf(modifier),
82           content = content
83       )
84   }
```

Figure 3.1 – Source code of Layout()

Layout() invokes ReusableComposeNode(), which belongs to the androidx.
compose.runtime package. This composable function *emits* a so-called **node**,
a UI element hierarchy. Nodes are created using a factory, which is passed through the
factory argument. The update and skippableUpdate parameters receive code that
performs updates on the node, with the latter one handling modifiers (we will be taking
a closer look at them at the end of this chapter). Finally, content contains composable
functions that become the children of the node.

> **Please Note**
>
> When we speak of composable functions *emitting* UI elements, we mean that
> **nodes** are added to data structures that are internal to Jetpack Compose. This
> will eventually lead to UI elements being visible.

To complete the call chain, let's briefly look at ReusableComposeNode():

```
411   @Composable @ExplicitGroupsComposable
412   inline fun <T, reified E : Applier<*>> ReusableComposeNode(
413       noinline factory: () → T,
414       update: @DisallowComposableCalls Updater<T>.() → Unit,
415       noinline skippableUpdate: @Composable SkippableUpdater<T>.() → Unit,
416       content: @Composable () → Unit
417   ) {
418       if (currentComposer.applier !is E) invalidApplier()
419       currentComposer.startReusableNode()
420       if (currentComposer.inserting) {
421           currentComposer.createNode(factory)
422       } else {
423           currentComposer.useNode()
424       }
425       currentComposer.disableReusing()
426       Updater<T>(currentComposer).update()
427       currentComposer.enableReusing()
428       SkippableUpdater<T>(currentComposer).skippableUpdate()
429       currentComposer.startReplaceableGroup( key: 0x7ab4aae9)
430       content()
431       currentComposer.endReplaceableGroup()
432       currentComposer.endNode()
433   }
```

Figure 3.2 – Source code of ReusableComposeNode()

currentComposer is a top-level variable inside androidx.compose.runtime. Composables.kt. Its type is Composer, which is an interface. Composer is targeted by the Jetpack Compose Kotlin compiler plugin and used by code generation helpers; your code should not call it directly. ReusableComposeNode determines if a new node should be created or whether an existing one should be reused. It then performs updates and finally emits the content to the node by invoking content().

Based on what you know by now, let me elaborate a little more on nodes. Layout() passes ComposeUiNode.Constructor to ReusableComposeNode as the factory argument, which is used to create a node (currentComposer. createNode(factory)). So, the features of a node are defined by the ComposeUiNode interface:

```
     Interface extracted from LayoutNode to not mark the whole LayoutNode class as @PublishedApi.
27   @PublishedApi
28   internal interface ComposeUiNode {
29       var measurePolicy: MeasurePolicy
30       var layoutDirection: LayoutDirection
31       var density: Density
32       var modifier: Modifier
33


     Object of pre-allocated lambdas used to make use with ComposeNode allocation-less.

37       companion object {
38           val Constructor: () -> ComposeUiNode = LayoutNode.Constructor
39           val SetModifier: ComposeUiNode.(Modifier) -> Unit = { this.modifier = it }
40           val SetDensity: ComposeUiNode.(Density) -> Unit = { this.density = it }
41           val SetMeasurePolicy: ComposeUiNode.(MeasurePolicy) -> Unit =
42               { this.measurePolicy = it }
43           val SetLayoutDirection: ComposeUiNode.(LayoutDirection) -> Unit =
44               { this.layoutDirection = it }
45       }
46   }
```

Figure 3.3 – Source code of ComposeUiNode

A node has four properties, as defined by the following classes or interfaces:

- MeasurePolicy
- LayoutDirection
- Density
- Modifier

In essence, a node is an element in a Compose hierarchy. You will not be dealing with them in your code because nodes are part of the inner workings of Jetpack Compose that are not exposed to apps. However, you will see `MeasurePolicy`, `LayoutDirection`, `Density`, and `Modifier` throughout this book. They represent important data structures and concepts that are relevant to apps.

This concludes our investigation of how UI elements are emitted (nodes are added to data structures that are internal to Jetpack Compose). In the next section, we will look at composable functions that return values.

Returning values

Most of your composable functions will not need to return something, so they will not specify a return type. This is because the main purpose of a composable is to compose the UI. As you saw in the previous section, this is done by emitting UI elements or element hierarchies. But when do we need to return something different than `Unit`?

Some of my examples invoke `remember {}` to retain state for future use and `stringResource()` to access strings that are stored in the `strings.xml` file. To be able to perform their tasks, both must be composable functions.

Let's look at `stringResource()` to see why. Remember that you can press Ctrl + click on a name to see its source code. The function is pretty short; it does just two things:

```
val resources = resources()
return resources.getString(id)
```

`resources()` is a composable too. It returns `LocalContext.current.resources`. `LocalContext` is a top-level variable in `AndroidCompositionLocals.android.kt` that belongs to the `androidx.compose.ui.platform` package. It returns an instance of `StaticProvidableCompositionLocal`, which holds `android.content.Context`. This object provides access to resources.

Even though the returned data has nothing to do with Jetpack Compose, the code that obtains it must conform to Jetpack Compose mechanics because, in the end, it will be called from a composable function. The important thing to remember is that if you need to return something that is part of the composition and recomposition mechanic, you must make your function composable by annotating it with `@Composable`. Also, such functions do not follow the naming conventions for composable functions but follow a *camelCase* style (they begin with a small letter, with the subsequent word starting in uppercase) and consist of verb phrases (`rememberScrollState`).

In the next section, we will return to composing UIs at the app level. You will learn more about the terms **composition** and **recomposition**.

Composing and recomposing the UI

Unlike imperative UI frameworks, Jetpack Compose does not depend on the developer proactively modifying a component tree when changes in the app data require changes to be made to the UI. Instead, Jetpack Compose detects such changes on its own and updates only the affected parts.

As you know by now, a Compose UI is declared *based on* the current app data. In my previous examples, you have seen quite a few conditional expressions (such as if or when) that determine which composable function is called or which parameters it receives. So, we are describing the *complete* UI in our code. The branch that will be executed depends on the app data (state) during runtime. The Web framework that React has a similar concept called Virtual DOM. But doesn't this contradict with me saying *Compose detects such changes on its own and updates only the affected parts*?

Conceptually, Jetpack Compose regenerates the entire UI when changes need to be applied. This, of course, would waste time, battery, and processing power. And it might be noticeable by the user as screen flickering. Therefore, the framework puts a lot of effort into making sure only those parts of the UI element tree requiring an update are regenerated.

You saw some of these efforts in the previous section, where I briefly mentioned update and skippableUpdate. To ensure fast and reliable **recompositions** (the Jetpack Compose term for updating, regenerating, or repainting), you need to make sure your composable functions follow a few simple rules. I will introduce them to you by walking you through the code of an app called ColorPickerDemo:

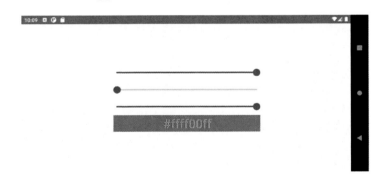

Figure 3.4 – The ColorPickerDemo app

The app aims to set a color by specifying its **red, green, and blue** (RGB) portions. This color is used as the background color of a text (which displays the value of the color as a hexadecimal string). The foreground color is complementary to the selected one.

In the next few sections, we look at its code. You will learn how sliders communicate changes in their values.

Sharing state among composable functions

Sometimes, you may want to use a state in more than one composable function. For example, you may wish to use the color portion that's been set by one slider to create the full color, which, in turn, becomes the background color of a text. So, how can you share state? Let's start by looking at ColorPicker() – it groups three sliders vertically in a Column():

```
@Composable
fun ColorPicker(color: MutableState<Color>) {
  val red = color.value.red
  val green = color.value.green
  val blue = color.value.blue
  Column {
    Slider(
      value = red,
      onValueChange = { color.value = Color(it, green,
                                            blue)
})
    Slider(
      value = green,
      onValueChange = { color.value = Color(red, it, blue) })
    Slider(
      value = blue,
      onValueChange = { color.value = Color(red, green, it) })
  }
}
```

The composable receives one parameter: `MutableState<Color>`. The `value` property of `color` contains an instance of `androidx.compose.ui.graphics.Color`. Its `red`, `green`, and `blue` properties return a `Float` based on the so-called **color space**, which is used to identify a specific organization of colors. Each color space is characterized by a color model, which, in turn, defines how a color value is represented. If not specified otherwise, this is `ColorSpaces.Srgb`.

My code does not set a particular color space, so it defaults to `ColorSpaces.Srgb`. This causes the value being returned to be between `0F` and `1F`. The first three lines assign the red, green, and blue portions of the color to local variables named `red`, `green`, and `blue`. They are used for the `Slider()` functions; let's see how.

Each slider in my example receives two parameters: `value` and `onValueChange`. The first specifies the value that the slider will display. It must be between `0F` and `1F` (which fits nicely with `red`, `green`, and `blue`). If needed, you can supply an alternative range through the optional `valueRange` parameter. `onValueChange` is invoked when the user drags the slider handle or clicks on the thin line underneath. The code of the three lambda expressions is quite similar: a new `Color` object is created and assigned to `color.value`. Color portions that are being controlled by other sliders are taken from the corresponding local variables. They have not been changed. The new color portion of the current slider can be obtained from `it` because it is the new slider value, which is passed to `onValueChange`.

By now, you may be wondering why `ColorPicker()` receives the color wrapped inside a `MutableState<Color>`. Wouldn't it suffice to pass it directly, using `color: Color`? As shown in *Figure 3.4*, the app shows the selected color as a text with complementary background and foreground colors. But `ColorPicker()` does not emit text. This happens somewhere else (as you will see shortly, inside a `Column()`). To show the correct color, the text must receive it too. As the color change takes place inside `ColorPicker()`, we must inform the caller about it. An ordinary `Color` instance being passed as a parameter can't do that because Kotlin function parameters are immutable.

We can achieve changeability using global properties. But this is not recommended for Jetpack Compose. Composables should not use global variables at all. It is a best practice to pass all the data that influences the look or behavior of a composable function as parameters. If that data is modified inside the composable, you should use `MutableState`. Moving state to a composable's caller by receiving a state is called **state hoisting**. A good alternative to passing `MutableState` and applying changes inside a composable is to pass the change logic as a lambda expression. In my example, `onValueChange` would just provide the new slider value to the lambda expression.

> **Important**
>
> Try to make your composables side effect-free. Having no side effects means
> calling a function repeatedly with the same set of arguments that will always
> produce the same result. Besides getting all the relevant data from the caller,
> being free of side effects also requires not relying on global properties or calling
> functions that return unpredictable values. There are a few scenarios where you
> want side effects. I will cover these in *Chapter 7, Tips, Tricks, and Best Practices*.

Now, let's learn how the color is passed to the text:

```
Column(
    modifier = Modifier.width(min(400.dp, maxWidth)),
    horizontalAlignment = Alignment.CenterHorizontally
) {
    val color = remember { mutableStateOf(Color.Magenta) }
    ColorPicker(color)
    Text(
        modifier = Modifier
            .fillMaxWidth()
            .background(color.value),
        text =
        "#${color.value.toArgb().toUInt().toString(16)}",
        textAlign = TextAlign.Center,
        style = MaterialTheme.typography.h4.merge(
            TextStyle(
                color = color.value.complementary()
            )
        )
    )
}
```

`ColorPicker()` and `Text()` are laid out vertically (being centered horizontally)
inside a `Column()`. The width of the column is either `400` density-independent pixels or
`maxWidth`, depending on which value is smaller. `maxWidth` is defined by the predefined
`BoxWithConstraints()` composable (you will learn more about it in the *Controlling
size* section). The color for both `ColorPicker()` and `Text()` is defined like this:

```
val color = remember { mutableStateOf(Color.Magenta) }
```

When `Column()` is composed for the first time, `mutableStateOf(Color.Magenta)` is executed. This creates **state**. State represents app data (in this case, a color) that changes over time. You will learn more about state in *Chapter 5, Managing the State of Your Composable Functions*. For now, it suffices to understand that the state is *remembered* and assigned to `color`.

But what does `remember` mean? Any subsequent composition, which is called **recomposition**, will lead to `color` receiving the value created by `mutableStateOf` – that is, a reference to a `MutableState<Color>` (state hoisting). The lambda expression that's passed to `remember` is called a **calculation**. It will only be evaluated once. Recompositions always return the same value.

If the reference remains the same, how can the color be changed? The actual color is accessed through the `value` property. You saw this in the code of `ColorPicker()`. `Text()` does not modify the color – it only works with it. Therefore, we pass `color.value` (which is the color), not the mutable state (`color`), to some of its parameters, such as `background`. Note that this is a modifier. You will learn more about them in the *Modifying behavior* section. It sets the background color of a UI element that's emitted by a composable function.

Also, have you noticed the call of `complementary()` inside `TextStyle()`? Here's what it does:

```
fun Color.complementary() = Color(
    red = 1F - red,
    green = 1F - green,
    blue = 1F - blue
)
```

`complementary()` is an extension function of `Color`. It computes the complementary color to the one it receives. This is done to make the text (the hexadecimal RGB value of the color that was selected using the three sliders) readable, regardless of the currently selected color (which is used as the background of the text).

In this section, I talked about some very important Jetpack Compose concepts. Let's recap what we've learned so far:

- A compose UI is defined by nesting calls to composable functions
- Composable functions emit UI elements or UI element hierarchies
- Building the UI for the first time is called **composition**

- Rebuilding the UI upon changes being made to app data is called **recomposition**
- Recomposition happens automatically

> **Important**
> There is no way for your app to predict when or how often recomposition will take place. If animations are involved, this may happen each frame. Therefore, it is of utmost importance to make your composables as fast as possible.
> You may never do time-consuming calculations, load or save data, or access the network. Any such code must be executed outside of composable functions. They only receive ready data. Also, please note that the order of recomposition is unspecified. This means that the first child of, say, a Column(), might be recomposed later than a sibling that appears after it in the source code. Recomposition can occur in parallel and it may be skipped. Therefore, never rely on a particular order of recomposition, and never compute something in a composable that is needed somewhere else.

In the next section, we will finish our walkthrough of the ColorPickerDemo app. I will show you how to specify and limit the dimensions of composable functions.

Controlling size

Most of my examples contain code such as fillMaxSize() or fillMaxWidth(). Both modifiers control the size of a composable. fillMaxSize() uses all the available horizontal and vertical space, while fillMaxWidth() maximizes only the horizontal expansion.

However, fillMaxWidth() may not be the right choice for sliders. In my opinion, large sliders are awkward to use due to the distance you would need to drag their handles to reach the minimum or maximum value. So, the question is, how can we limit its width? The most straightforward solution is to use the width() modifier. It sets the preferred width of a composable to a particular size. I want sliders to be 400 density-independent pixels wide at most. If the screen is smaller, its width should be used instead. Here's how you achieve this:

```
modifier = Modifier.width(min(400.dp, maxWidth)),
```

The modifier belongs to the Column() property that contains both ColorPicker() and Text().

maxWidth is provided by the BoxWithConstraints() composable:

```
BoxWithConstraints(
    contentAlignment = Alignment.Center,
    modifier = Modifier.fillMaxSize()
) {
    Column ...
}
```

Its content receives an instance of a BoxWithConstraintsScope scope, which provides access to constraints, minWidth, minHeight, maxWidth, and maxHeight. BoxWithConstraints() defines its content according to the available space, based on incoming constraints. You will learn more about this in *Chapter 4, Laying Out UI Elements*.

This concludes our walkthrough of the ColorPickerDemo app. In the next section, we take a closer look at how a composable hierarchy is displayed in an Activity.

Displaying a composable hierarchy inside an Activity

In the previous section, we built a UI element hierarchy consisting of three sliders and some text. We embedded it in an Activity using setContent, an extension function of androidx.activity.ComponentActivity. This implies that you cannot invoke setContent on *any* activity, but only ones that extend ComponentActivty. This is the case for androidx.appcompat.app.AppCompatActivity.

However, this class inherits quite a lot of functionality that is relevant for the old View-based world, such as support for toolbars and the options menu. Jetpack Compose handles these differently. You will learn more about this in *Chapter 6, Putting Pieces Together*. Therefore, you should avoid using AppCompatActivity, and instead extend ComponentActivity if possible. For combining View-based and Compose UIs, please refer to *Chapter 9, Exploring Interoperability APIs*.

Let's return to setContent. It expects two parameters:

- parent, an optional CompositionContext
- content, a composable function for declaring the UI

You will likely omit `parent` most of the time. `CompositionContext` is an abstract class that belongs to the `androidx.compose.runtime` package. It is used to logically connect two compositions. This refers to the inner workings of Jetpack Compose that you do not need to worry about in your app code. Yet, to get an idea of what this means, let's look at the source code of `setContent`:

```
48    public fun ComponentActivity.setContent(
49        parent: CompositionContext? = null,
50        content: @Composable () → Unit
51    ) {
52        val existingComposeView = window.decorView
53            .findViewById<ViewGroup>(android.R.id.content)
54            .getChildAt( index: 0) as? ComposeView
55
56        if (existingComposeView ≠ null) with(existingComposeView) {  this: ComposeView
57            setParentCompositionContext(parent)
58            setContent(content)
59        } else ComposeView( context: this).apply {  this: ComposeView
60            // Set content and parent **before** setContentView
61            // to have ComposeView create the composition on attach
62            setParentCompositionContext(parent)
63            setContent(content)
64            // Set the view tree owners before setting the content view so that the inflation process
65            // and attach listeners will see them already present
66            setOwners()
67            setContentView( view: this, DefaultActivityContentLayoutParams)
68        }
69    }
```

Figure 3.5 – The source code of setContent

First, `findViewById()` is used to find out if the activity already contains content that is an instance of `androidx.compose.ui.platform.ComposeView`. If so, the `setParentCompositionContext()` and `setContent()` methods of this view will be invoked.

Let's look at `setParentCompositionContext()` first. It belongs to `AbstractComposeView`, the immediate parent of `ComposeView`. It sets a `CompositionContext` that should be the parent of the view's composition. If that context is `null`, it will be determined automatically: `AbstractComposeView` contains a private function called `ensureCompositionCreated()`. It invokes another implementation of `setContent` (an internal extension function of `ViewGroup` that's defined in `Wrapper.android.kt`) and passes the result of a call to `resolveParentCompositionContext()` as a `parent`.

Now, let's return to the version of `setContent()` that's shown in the preceding screenshot. Once `setParentCompositionContext()` has been called, it invokes yet another version of `setContent()`. This implementation belongs to `ComposeView`. It sets the content of the view.

If `findViewById()` does not return a `ComposeView`, a new instance is created and passed to `setContentView`, after `setParentCompositionContext()` and `setContent()` have been invoked.

In this section, we continued looking at some of the inner workings of Jetpack Compose. You now know that `ComposeView` is the missing link to the old-fashioned View-based world. We will revisit this class in *Chapter 9, Exploring Interoperability APIs*.

In the next section, we will return modifiers; you will learn how they work under the hood and how you can write your own.

Modifying the behavior of composable functions

Unlike components in traditional imperative UI frameworks, composable functions do not share a basic set of properties. They also do not automatically (in the sense of inheriting) reuse functionality. This must be done explicitly by calling other composables. Their visual appearance and behavior can be controlled through parameters, modifiers, or both. In a way, modifiers pick up the idea of properties in a component but enhance it – unlike properties of components, modifiers can be used completely at the discretion of the developer.

You have already seen quite a few modifiers in my examples, such as the following:

- `width()`
- `fillMaxWidth()`
- `fillMaxSize()`

These control the width and size of the corresponding UI element; `background()` can set a background color and shape, while `clickable {}` allows the user to interact with the composable function by clicking on the UI element. Jetpack Compose provides an extensive list of modifiers, so it may take some time to make yourself familiar with most of them. Conceptually, these modifiers can be assigned to one of several categories, such as *Actions* (`draggable()`), *Alignment* (`alignByBaseline()`), or *Drawing* (`paint()`). You can find a list of modifiers grouped by category at `https://developer.android.com/jetpack/compose/modifiers-list`.

To further familiarize yourself with modifiers, let's look at the `ModifierDemo` example. It contains several composable functions. The following screenshot shows the app running `OrderDemo()`:

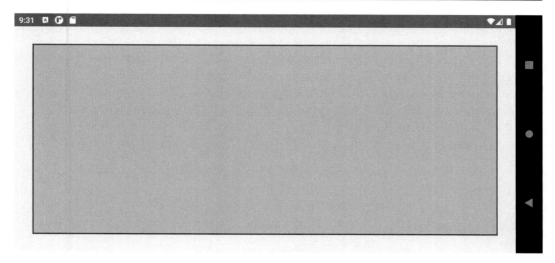

Figure 3.6 – The ModifierDemo app

The composable produces a gap of 32 density-independent pixels on all its sides, followed by a 2 density-independent pixels wide blue border. The inner rectangle is painted in light gray.

Here's what the code looks like:

```
@Composable
fun OrderDemo() {
  var color by remember { mutableStateOf(Color.Blue) }
  Box(
    modifier = Modifier
      .fillMaxSize()
      .padding(32.dp)
      .border(BorderStroke(width = 2.dp, color = color))
      .background(Color.LightGray)
      .clickable {
        color = if (color == Color.Blue)
          Color.Red
        else
          Color.Blue
      }
  )
}
```

`Box()` is clickable – doing so changes the border color from blue to red and back. If you click inside the gaps, nothing will happen. If, however, you move `.clickable { }` before `.padding(32.dp)`, clicks work inside the gaps too. This is intentional. Here's what happens: you define a modifier chain by combining several modifiers with `.`. In doing so, you specify the order in which the modifiers are used. The location of a modifier in the chain determines when it is executed. As `clickable {}` only reacts to clicks inside the bounds of a composable, the padding is not considered for clicks when it occurs before `clickable {}`.

In the next section, I will show you how Jetpack Compose handles modifiers and modifier chains internally.

Understanding how modifiers work

Composable functions that accept modifiers should receive them via the `modifier` parameter and assign it a default value of `Modifier`. `modifier` should be the first optional parameter and thus appear after all the required ones, except for trailing lambda parameters.

Let's see how a composable can receive a `modifier` parameter:

```
@Composable
fun TextWithYellowBackground(
  text: String,
  modifier: Modifier = Modifier
) {
  Text(
    text = text,
    modifier = modifier.background(Color.Yellow)
  )
}
```

This way, the composable can receive a modifier chain from the caller. If none are provided, `Modifier` acts as a new, empty chain. In both cases, the composable can add additional modifiers, such as `background()` in the previous code snippet.

If a composable function accepts a modifier that will be applied to a specific part or child of its corresponding UI element, the name of this part or child should be used as a prefix, such as `titleModifier`. Such modifiers follow the rules I mentioned previously. They should be grouped and appear after the parent's modifier. Please refer to `https://developer.android.com/reference/kotlin/androidx/compose/ui/Modifier` for additional information regarding the definition of modifier parameters.

Now that you know how to define a `modifier` parameter in a composable function, let's focus a little more on the idea of chaining. `Modifier` is both an interface and a companion object. The interface belongs to the `androidx.compose.ui` package. It defines several functions, such as `foldIn()` and `foldOut()`. You won't need them, though. The important one is `then()`. It concatenates two modifiers. As you will see shortly, you need to invoke it in your modifiers. The `Element` interface extends `Modifier`. It defines a single element contained within a `Modifier` chain. Finally, the `Modifier` companion object is the empty, default modifier, which contains no elements.

To Summarize

A modifier is an ordered, immutable collection of modifier elements.

Next, let's see how the `background()` modifier is implemented:

```
Draws shape with a solid color behind the content.

Params:   color - color to paint background with
          shape - desired shape of the background

Samples: androidx.compose.foundation.samples.DrawBackgroundColor
         // Unresolved

42    fun Modifier.background(
43        color: Color,
44        shape: Shape = RectangleShape
45    ) = this.then(
46        Background(
47            color = color,
48            shape = shape,
49            inspectorInfo = debugInspectorInfo {   this: InspectorInfo
50                name = "background"
51                value = color
52                properties["color"] = color
53                properties["shape"] = shape
54            }
55        )
56    )
```

Figure 3.7 – Source code of the background() modifier

background() is an extension function of Modifier. It receives a Modifier instance. It invokes then() and returns the result (a concatenated modifier). then() expects just one parameter: the *other* modifier that should be concatenated with the current one. In the case of background(), *other* is an instance of Background. This class extends InspectorValueInfo and implements the DrawModifier interface, which, in turn, extends Modifier.Element. As InspectorValueInfo is primarily used for debugging purposes, I will not elaborate on it any further. DrawModifier, on the other hand, is very interesting. Implementations can draw into the space of a UI element. We will make use of this in the final section.

Implementing custom modifiers

Although Jetpack Compose contains an extensive list of modifiers, you may want to implement your own. Let me show you how to do this. My example, drawYellowCross(), draws two thick yellow lines behind the content, which is some Text() here:

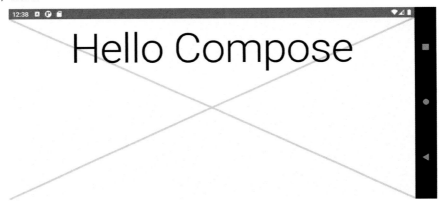

Figure 3.8 – A custom modifier

The modifier is invoked like this:

```
Text(
  text = "Hello Compose",
  modifier = Modifier
    .fillMaxSize()
    .drawYellowCross(),
  textAlign = TextAlign.Center,
  style = MaterialTheme.typography.h1
)
```

As you can see, the modifier integrates nicely into an existing modifier chain. Now, let's look at the source code:

```
fun Modifier.drawYellowCross() = then(
  object : DrawModifier {
    override fun ContentDrawScope.draw() {
      drawLine(
        color = Color.Yellow,
        start = Offset(0F, 0F),
        end = Offset(size.width - 1, size.height - 1),
        strokeWidth = 10F
      )
      drawLine(
        color = Color.Yellow,
        start = Offset(0F, size.height - 1),
        end = Offset(size.width - 1, 0F),
        strokeWidth = 10F
      )
      drawContent()
    }
  }
)
```

drawYellowCross() is an extension function of Modifier. This means we can invoke then() and simply return the result. then() receives an instance of DrawModifier. After that, we need to implement only one function, called draw(), which is an extension function of ContentDrawScope. This interface defines one function (drawContent()) and extends DrawScope; this way, we gain access to quite a few drawing primitives, such as drawLine(), drawRect(), and drawImage(). drawContent() draws the UI element, so depending on when it is invoked, the element appears in front of, or behind, the other drawing primitives. In my example, it is the last instruction, so the UI element (for example, Text()) is the topmost one.

Jetpack Compose also includes a modifier called drawBehind {}. It receives a lambda expression that can contain drawing primitives, just like in my example. To learn even more about the internals of Jetpack Compose, you may want to take a look at its source code. To see it, just click on drawBehind() in your code while pressing the *Ctrl* key.

This concludes my explanations of modifiers. As you have seen, they are a very elegant way to control both the visual appearance and behavior of composable functions.

Summary

This chapter introduced you to the key principles of Jetpack Compose. We closely looked at the underlying ideas and concepts of composable functions, and you now know how they are written and used. We also focused on how to create and update the UI, as well as how Jetpack Compose achieves what other frameworks call repainting or updating the screen. When relevant app data changes, the UI changes, or so-called recomposition takes place automatically, this is one of the advantages over the traditional View-based approach, where the developer must imperatively change the component tree.

We then expanded our knowledge of the concept of modifiers. We looked at how modifier chains work and what you need to keep in mind to always get the intended results. For example, to receive clicks inside padding, `padding {}` must occur after `clickable {}` in the `modifier` chain. Finally, you learned how to implement custom modifiers.

In *Chapter 4, Laying Out UI Elements*, we will examine how to lay out UI elements and introduce you to the **single measure pass**. We will explore built-in layouts, but also write a custom Compose layout.

Part 2: Building User Interfaces

This part takes a practical approach to teach you how to write fast, robust, and beautiful Jetpack Compose apps. The many examples will provide you with a solid understanding of how the library works.

We will cover the following chapters in this section:

- *Chapter 4, Laying Out UI Elements*
- *Chapter 5, Managing the State of Your Composable Functions*
- *Chapter 6, Putting Pieces Together*
- *Chapter 7, Tips, Tricks, and Best Practices*

4

Laying Out UI Elements

In the previous chapters, you learned how to build simple UIs. Although they consisted of just a few UI elements, they needed to arrange their buttons, text fields, and sliders in a particular order, direction, or hierarchy. **Layouts** position and size their content in a way specific to this layout, such as horizontally (Row()) or vertically (Column()). This chapter explores layouts in greater detail.

In this chapter, we will cover the following topics:

- Using predefined layouts
- Understanding the single measure pass
- Creating custom layouts

We will start by exploring the predefined layouts of Row(), Column(), and Box(). You will learn how to combine them to create beautiful UIs. Next, I'll introduce you to ConstraintLayout. It places composables that are relative to others on the screen and uses attributes to flatten the UI element hierarchy. This is an alternative to nesting Row(), Column(), and Box().

The second main section will explain why the layout system in Jetpack Compose is more performant than the traditional View-based approach. We will once again go under the covers and look at some of the internals of the Compose runtime. This will prepare you for the final main section of this chapter, *Creating custom layouts*.

In this final section, you will learn how to create a custom layout and thus gain precise control over the rendering of its children. This is helpful if the predefined layouts do not offer enough flexibility for a particular use case.

Now, let's get started!

Technical requirements

This chapter showcases three sample apps:

- `PredefinedLayoutsDemo`
- `ConstraintLayoutDemo`
- `CustomLayoutDemo`

Please refer to the *Technical requirements* section of *Chapter 1, Building Your First Compose App*, for information about how to install and set up Android Studio, and how to get it. If you want to try the `CheckboxWithLabel()` composable from the *Combining basic building blocks* section, you can use the *Sandbox* app project in the top-level directory of this book's GitHub repository at `https://github.com/PacktPublishing/Android-UI-Development-with-Jetpack-Compose`. Open its `SandboxActivity` and copy the composable functions from `code_snippets.txt`, which is located in the `/chapter_04` folder.

Using predefined layouts

When you create a UI, you must define where its elements appear and how big they are. Jetpack Compose provides a couple of basic layouts, which arrange their content along one main axis. There are three axes to consider:

- Horizontal
- Vertical
- Stacked

Each axis is represented by a layout. Row() arranges its content horizontally, while Column() does so vertically. Box() and BoxWithConstraints() stack their contents on top of each other. By combining these axis-orientated building blocks, you can create great-looking UIs easily.

Combining basic building blocks

The following PredefinedLayoutsDemo sample app shows three checkboxes that toggle a red, a green, and a blue rectangle, respectively. The boxes appear only if the corresponding checkbox is checked:

Figure 4.1 – The sample PredefinedLayoutsDemo app

Let's see how this is done. First, I will show you how to create a checkbox with an accompanying label:

```
@Composable
fun CheckboxWithLabel(label: String, state:
MutableState<Boolean>) {
  Row(
    modifier = Modifier.clickable {
      state.value = !state.value
    }, verticalAlignment = Alignment.CenterVertically
  ) {
    Checkbox(
      checked = state.value,
      onCheckedChange = {
```

```
        state.value = it
      }
    )
  Text(
    text = label,
    modifier = Modifier.padding(start = 8.dp)
  )
  }
}
```

Jetpack Compose has a built-in `Checkbox()`. It receives the current state (`checked`) and a lambda expression (`onCheckedChange`), which is invoked when the checkbox is clicked. At the time of writing, you cannot pass a label. However, we can achieve something similar by putting `Checkbox()` and `Text()` inside a `Row()`. We need to make the row clickable because we want to change the state of the checkbox when the text is clicked too. To make the checkbox with a label more visually appealing, we can center `Checkbox()` and `Text()` vertically inside the row by setting `verticalAlignment` to `Alignment.CenterVertically`.

`CheckboxWithLabel()` receives a `MutableState<Boolean>` because other composables need to be recomposed when it changes the value inside `onCheckedChange`.

Next, let's see where the state is created:

```
@Composable
fun PredefinedLayoutsDemo() {
  val red = remember { mutableStateOf(true) }
  val green = remember { mutableStateOf(true) }
  val blue = remember { mutableStateOf(true) }
  Column(
    modifier = Modifier
      .fillMaxSize()
      .padding(16.dp)
  ) {
    …
```

`PredefinedLayoutsDemo()` arranges its content vertically by putting it inside a `Column()`. The column fills all the available space (`fillMaxSize()`) and has a padding of 16 density-independent pixels on all four sides (`padding(16.dp)`). The three states (`red`, `green`, and `blue`) are passed to `CheckboxWithLabel()`. Here's what these invocations look like:

```
CheckboxWithLabel(
    label = stringResource(id = R.string.red),
    state = red
)
CheckboxWithLabel(
    label = stringResource(id = R.string.green),
    state = green
)
CheckboxWithLabel(
    label = stringResource(id = R.string.blue),
    state = blue
)
```

They are almost the same, differing only in the state (`red`, `green`, and `blue`) and the label string (`R.string.red`, `R.string.green`, or `R.string.blue`).

Now, let's find out how the stacked colored boxes are created:

```
Box(
    modifier = Modifier
        .fillMaxSize()
        .padding(top = 16.dp)
) {
    if (red.value) {
        Box(
            modifier = Modifier
                .fillMaxSize()
                .background(Color.Red)
        )
    }
    if (green.value) {
        Box(
            modifier = Modifier
```

```
        .fillMaxSize()
        .padding(32.dp)
        .background(Color.Green)
    )
  }
  if (blue.value) {
    Box(
      modifier = Modifier
        .fillMaxSize()
        .padding(64.dp)
        .background(Color.Blue)
    )
  }
}
```

The three colored boxes are put inside another `Box()`, which fills all the available space. To create a gap between it and the last checkbox, I specified a top padding of 16 density-independent pixels.

A colored box is only added if its corresponding state is `true` (for example, `if (red.value) { ...)`. All colored boxes fill the available space. As they will be stacked on top of each other, only the last (top) one will be visible. To fix this, the green and blue boxes receive paddings that differ in size: the padding for the blue box (the last one) is 64 density-independent pixels, so in the areas of the padding, the green box becomes visible. The green box has a padding of 32 density-independent pixels, so in this area, the first box (the red one) can be seen.

As you have seen, by combining basic layouts such as `Box()` and `Row()`, you can easily create great-looking UIs. In the next section, I will introduce you to an alternative approach where we will define a UI based on constraints.

Creating layouts based on constraints

Defining UIs based on constraints has been the most recent preferred approach in Android's traditional `View` world because older layouts such as `RelativeLayout` or `LinearLayout` could impact performance when they're used in large, multiply-nested layouts. `ConstraintLayout` avoids this by flattening the `View` hierarchy. As you will see in the *Understanding the single measure pass* section, this is no issue for Jetpack Compose.

However, for more complex layouts in a Compose app, you may still want to limit the nesting of Box(), Row(), and Column() to make your code simpler and clearer. This is where ConstraintLayout() can help.

The ConstraintLayoutDemo sample app is a reimplementation of PredefinedLayoutsDemo based on ConstraintLayout(). By comparing the two versions, you get a thorough understanding of how this composable function works. To use ConstraintLayout() in your app, you need to add a dependency to your module-level build.gradle file. Please note that the version number shown here is just an example. You can find the latest version at https://developer.android.com/jetpack/androidx/versions/all-channel:

```
implementation "androidx.constraintlayout:constraintlayout-
compose:1.0.0-rc02"
```

So, how do we define a layout based on constraints? Let's find out by examining the reimplementation of CheckboxWithLabel(). It places text next to a checkbox:

```
@Composable
fun CheckboxWithLabel(
  label: String,
  state: MutableState<Boolean>,
  modifier: Modifier = Modifier
) {
  ConstraintLayout(modifier = modifier.clickable {
    state.value = !state.value
  }) {
    val (checkbox, text) = createRefs()
    Checkbox(
      checked = state.value,
      onCheckedChange = {
        state.value = it
      },
      modifier = Modifier.constrainAs(checkbox) {
      }
    )
    Text(
      text = label,
      modifier = Modifier.constrainAs(text) {
```

```
        start.linkTo(checkbox.end, margin = 8.dp)
        top.linkTo(checkbox.top)
        bottom.linkTo(checkbox.bottom)
      }
    )
  }
}
```

`ConstraintLayout()` uses a **domain-specific language (DSL)** to define the location and size of a UI element relative to other ones. Therefore, each composable in a `ConstraintLayout()` must have a reference associated with it, which is created using `createRefs()`. Constraints are provided using the `constrainAs()` modifier. Its lambda expression receives a `ConstrainScope`. It includes properties such as `start`, `top`, and `bottom`. These are called **anchors** because they define a location that can be linked (using `linkTo()`) to the location of another composable.

Let's look at `Text()`. Its `constrainAs()` contains `bottom.linkTo(checkbox.bottom)`. This means that the bottom of the text is constrained to the bottom of the checkbox. As the top of the text is linked to the top of the checkbox, the height of the text is equal to the height of the checkbox. The following line means that the start of the text is constrained by the end of the checkbox, with an additional margin of 8 density-independent pixels:

```
start.linkTo(checkbox.end, margin = 8.dp)
```

So, in the direction of reading, the text comes after the checkbox. Next, let's look at `ConstraintLayoutDemo()`:

```
@Composable
fun ConstraintLayoutDemo() {
  val red = remember { mutableStateOf(true) }
  val green = remember { mutableStateOf(true) }
  val blue = remember { mutableStateOf(true) }
  ConstraintLayout(
    modifier = Modifier
      .fillMaxSize()
      .padding(16.dp)
  ) {
    val (cbRed, cbGreen, cbBlue, boxRed, boxGreen, boxBlue) =
        createRefs()
```

```
CheckboxWithLabel(
    label = stringResource(id = R.string.red),
    state = red,
    modifier = Modifier.constrainAs(cbRed) {
        top.linkTo(parent.top)
    }
)
...
```

Once we have created the references that are needed to define constraints using `createRefs()`, we add our first `CheckboxWithLabel()`. Its `top` is linked to (constrained by) the `top` of `parent`, which is `ConstraintLayout()`. So, the first checkbox with a label is the topmost one. Here's how the second one, which toggles the green box, is invoked:

```
CheckboxWithLabel(
    label = stringResource(id = R.string.green),
    state = green,
    modifier = Modifier.constrainAs(cbGreen) {
        top.linkTo(cbRed.bottom)
    }
)
```

Its top is constrained by the bottom of the first checkbox with a label (which toggles the red box). Finally, here's how we need to constrain the third `CheckboxWithLabel()`:

```
modifier = Modifier.constrainAs(cbBlue) {
    top.linkTo(cbGreen.bottom)
}
```

To conclude this section, let me show you how to define the colored boxes. Here's the red one:

```
if (red.value) {
    Box(
        modifier = Modifier
            .background(Color.Red)
            .constrainAs(boxRed) {
                start.linkTo(parent.start)
```

```
        end.linkTo(parent.end)
        top.linkTo(cbBlue.bottom, margin = 16.dp)
        bottom.linkTo(parent.bottom)
        width = Dimension.fillToConstraints
        height = Dimension.fillToConstraints
    }
  )
}
```

Both `start` and `end` are linked to the corresponding anchors of `parent` (which is `ConstraintLayout()`). `top` is constrained by `bottom` of the last checkbox, so the red box appears below it. `bottom` of the red box is constrained by `bottom` of `parent`. Please note that currently, we must set `width` and `height` to the value that we obtained from `Dimension.fillToConstraints`. Otherwise, the box won't have the correct size.

Next, let's look at the constraints of the green box:

```
constrainAs(boxGreen) {
  start.linkTo(parent.start, margin = 32.dp)
  end.linkTo(parent.end, margin = 32.dp)
  top.linkTo(cbBlue.bottom, margin = (16 + 32).dp)
  bottom.linkTo(parent.bottom, margin = 32.dp)
  width = Dimension.fillToConstraints
  height = Dimension.fillToConstraints
}
```

This code is practically the same. One difference is that all the sides receive a `margin` of 32 density-independent pixels. This is necessary because we want the red box, which is below the green one, to be visible at the locations of the margin. As the red box already has a `top` margin of 16, we must add this value to the `top` margin. You may be wondering why I am not linking to `boxRed` instead. That is because the red box will not be present if its corresponding checkbox is not checked. In this case, the anchor would not be there.

Here's what the constraints for the blue box will look like:

```
constrainAs(boxBlue) {
  start.linkTo(parent.start, margin = 64.dp)
  end.linkTo(parent.end, margin = 64.dp)
  top.linkTo(cbBlue.bottom, margin = (16 + 64).dp)
```

```
  bottom.linkTo(parent.bottom, margin = 64.dp)
  width = Dimension.fillToConstraints
  height = Dimension.fillToConstraints
}
```

The only thing I needed to change is the margin on all four sides because otherwise, the box below (the green one) would not be visible.

In a nutshell, this is how `ConstrainLayout()` works:

- You constrain a composable by linking its anchors to other ones
- The linking is based on references. To setup these references, you must call `createRefs()`.

The main advantage of combining `Box()`, `Row()`, and `Column()` is that you flatten your UI element hierarchy. Think of it like this: in `PredefinedLayoutsDemo`, I needed to stack the colored boxes in a parent `Box()`. In `ConstrainLayoutDemo`, the boxes and the three `CheckboxWithLabel()` share the same parent (a `ConstrainLayout()`). This reduces the number of composables and makes the code cleaner.

In the next section, we will once again peek inside the internals of Jetpack Compose. We will learn how the layout process works and why it is more efficient than the traditional View-based approach.

Understanding the single measure pass

Laying out a UI element hierarchy means determining the sizes of all the elements and positioning them on the screen based on the layout strategy of their parent. At first, getting the size of, say, some text doesn't sound too complicated. After all, isn't it determined by the font and the text to be output? Here's an example, with two pieces of text laid out in a `Column()`:

```
@Composable
@Preview
fun ColumnWithTexts() {
  Column {
    Text(
      text = "Android UI development with Jetpack Compose",
      style = MaterialTheme.typography.h3
    )
    Text(
```

```
        text = "Hello Compose",
        style = MaterialTheme
            .typography.h5.merge(TextStyle(color = Color.Red))
    )
  }
}
```

If you deploy the preview, you will notice that, in portrait mode, the first text requires more space vertically than in landscape mode. The second text always fits into one line. The size that a composable takes on-screen partially depends on the conditions that have been imposed from *outside*. Here, the maximum width of the column (the parent) influences the height of the first piece of text. Such conditions are called **constraints**. You will see them in action in the *Creating custom layouts* section. Please note that they are not the same as the constraints you use in ConstraintLayout().

Once a layout has obtained and measured the size of its content, the layout will position its children (the content). Let's see how this works by looking at the source code of Column():

```
65   @Composable
66   inline fun Column(
67       modifier: Modifier = Modifier,
68       verticalArrangement: Arrangement.Vertical = Arrangement.Top,
69       horizontalAlignment: Alignment.Horizontal = Alignment.Start,
70       content: @Composable ColumnScope.() → Unit
71   ) {
72       val measurePolicy = columnMeasurePolicy(verticalArrangement, horizontalAlignment)
73       Layout(
74           content = { ColumnScopeInstance.content() },
75           measurePolicy = measurePolicy,
76           modifier = modifier
77       )
78   }
```

Figure 4.2 – Source code of Column()

The composable is very short. Besides assigning a value to measurePolicy, it only invokes Layout(), passing content, measurePolicy, and modifier. We briefly looked at the source code of Layout() in the *Emitting UI elements* section of *Chapter 3, Exploring the Key Principles of Compose*, to understand what it means to emit UI elements. Now, we'll focus on the layout process. The measurePolicy variable references an implementation of the MeasurePolicy interface. In this case, it's the result of a call to columnMeasurePolicy().

Defining measure policies

Depending on the values of `verticalArrangement` and `horizontalAlignment`, the call to `columnMeasurePolicy()` returns either `DefaultColumnMeasurePolicy` (a variable) or the result of `rowColumnMeasurePolicy()`. `DefaultColumnMeasurePolicy` calls `rowColumnMeasurePolicy`. Therefore, this function defines the measure policy for any `Column()`. It returns a `MeasurePolicy`.

> **Tip**
> Please remember that you can look at the source code of a policy by pressing the *Ctrl* key and clicking on a name, such as `columnMeasurePolicy`.

`MeasurePolicy` belongs to the `androidx.compose.ui.layout` package. It defines how a layout is measured and laid out, so it is the main building block for both predefined (for example, `Box()`, `Row()`, and `Column()`) and custom layouts. Its most important function is `measure()`, which is an extension function of `MeasureScope`. This function receives two parameters, `List<Measurable>` and `Constraints`. The elements of the list represent the children of the layout. They can be measured using `Measurable.measure()`. This function returns an instance of `Placeable`, a representation of the size a child wants to span.

`MeasureScope.measure()` returns an instance of `MeasureResult`. This interface defines the following components:

- The size of a layout (`width`, `height`)
- Alignment lines (`alignmentLines`)
- Logic to position the children (`placeChildren()`)

You can find an implementation of `MeasureResult` in the *Creating custom layouts* section.

Alignment lines define an offset line that can be used by parent layouts to align and position their children. For example, text baselines are alignment lines.

Depending on the complexity of the UI, a layout may find that its children do not fit nicely in its boundaries. The layout may want to remeasure the children, passing different measurement configurations. Remeasuring children is possible in the Android `View` system, but this can lead to decreased performance. Therefore, in Jetpack Compose, a layout may measure its content only once. If it tries again, an exception will be thrown.

A layout can, however, query the **intrinsic size** of its children and use it for sizing and positioning. MeasurePolicy defines four extension functions of IntrinsicMeasureScope. minIntrinsicWidth() and maxIntrinsicWidth() return the minimum or maximum width of a layout, given a particular height, so that the content of the layout can be painted completely. minIntrinsicHeight() and maxIntrinsicHeight() return the minimum or maximum height of a layout given a particular width so that the content of the layout can be painted completely. To get an idea of how they work, let's briefly look at one of them:

```
       The function used to calculate IntrinsicMeasurable.minIntrinsicWidth. It represents the minimum width this
       layout can take, given a specific height, such that the content of the layout can be painted correctly.
94    fun IntrinsicMeasureScope.minIntrinsicWidth(
95        measurables: List<IntrinsicMeasurable>,
96        height: Int
97    ): Int {
98        val mapped = measurables.fastMap {
99            DefaultIntrinsicMeasurable(it, IntrinsicMinMax.Min, IntrinsicWidthHeight.Width)
100        }
101        val constraints = Constraints(maxHeight = height)
102        val layoutReceiver = IntrinsicsMeasureScope( density: this, layoutDirection)
103        val layoutResult = layoutReceiver.measure(mapped, constraints)
104        return layoutResult.width
105    }
```

Figure 4.3 – Source code of minIntrinsicWidth()

IntrinsicMeasureScope.minIntrinsicWidth() receives two parameters: height and a list of children (measurables). The IntrinsicMeasurable interface defines four functions that obtain the minimum or maximum values for a particular element (minIntrinsicWidth(), maxIntrinsicWidth(), minIntrinsicHeight(), and maxIntrinsicHeight()). Each element of measurables is converted into an instance of DefaultIntrinsicMeasurable. As this class implements the Measurable interface, it provides an implementation of measure(). It returns FixedSizeIntrinsicsPlaceable, which provides the smallest possible width for a given height. The converted children are measured by an instance of IntrinsicsMeasureScope.

We'll finish looking at the internals of the Compose layout process by turning to Constraints. They are, for example, passed to MeasureScope.measure(). The class belongs to the androidx.compose.ui.unit package. It stores four values: minWidth, minHeight, maxWidth, and maxHeight. They define the minimum and maximum values the children of a layout must honor when measuring themselves. So, their width must be no smaller than minWidth and no larger than maxWidth. Their height must lie within minHeight and maxHeight.

The companion object defines the `Infinity` constant. It is used to signal that the constraint should be considered infinite. To create a `Constraints` instance, you can invoke the top-level `Constraints()` function.

This was a lot of information. Before moving on, let's recap what we have learned.

- The `Layout()` composable receives three parameters: the content, the measure policy, and a modifier.
- The measure policy defines how a layout is measured and laid out.
- The intrinsic size of a layout determines the minimum or maximum dimension for the corresponding input.

In the traditional View system, a parent view may call the `measure()` method more than once on its children (please refer to `https://developer.android.com/guide/topics/ui/how-android-draws` for details). On the other hand, Jetpack Compose requires that children must be measured *exactly once* before they are positioned. This results in a more performant measurement.

In the next section, we will make use of this knowledge by implementing a simple custom layout. It will position its children from left to right and from top to bottom. When one row is filled, the next one will be started below it.

Creating custom layouts

Sometimes, you may want to lay children out one after another in a row and start a new row when the current one has been filled. The `CustomLayoutDemo` sample app, as shown in the following screenshot, shows you how to do this. It creates 43 randomly colored boxes that vary in width and height:

Figure 4.4 – Sample CustomLayoutDemo app

Let's start by looking at the composable function that creates colored boxes:

```
@Composable
fun ColoredBox() {
  Box(
    modifier = Modifier
      .border(
        width = 2.dp,
        color = Color.Black
      )
      .background(randomColor())
      .width((40 * randomInt123()).dp)
      .height((10 * randomInt123()).dp)
  )
}
```

A colored box consists of a `Box()` with a black, two density-independent pixels wide border. The `width()` and `height()` modifiers set the preferred size of the box. This means that the layout could override it. For simplicity, my example doesn't. `randomInt123()` randomly returns either 1, 2, or 3:

```
private fun randomInt123() = Random.nextInt(1, 4)
```

`randomColor()` randomly returns red, green, or blue:

```
private fun randomColor() = when (randomInt123()) {
    1 -> Color.Red
    2 -> Color.Green
    else -> Color.Blue
}
```

Next, I'll show you how the colored boxes are created and set as the content of my custom layout:

```
@Composable
@Preview
fun CustomLayoutDemo() {
    SimpleFlexBox {
        for (i in 0..42) {
            ColoredBox()
```

```
        }
      }
}
```

`SimpleFlexBox()` is our custom layout. It is used like any predefined layout. You can even provide a modifier (which has not been done here for simplicity). So, how does the custom layout work? Let's find out:

```
@Composable
fun SimpleFlexBox(
    modifier: Modifier = Modifier,
    content: @Composable () -> Unit
) {
    Layout(
        modifier = modifier,
        content = content,
        measurePolicy = simpleFlexboxMeasurePolicy()
    )
}
```

Custom layouts should receive at least two parameters – `content` and a `modifier` with a default value of `Modifier`. Additional parameters may influence the behavior of your custom layout. For example, you may want to make the alignment of children configurable. For simplicity, the example does not do so.

As you know from the previous section, measurement and positioning are defined through a measure policy. I will show you how to implement one in the next section.

Implementing a custom measure policy

At this point, I have shown you almost all the code for the custom layout. The only thing that's missing is the measure policy. Let's see how it works:

```
private fun simpleFlexboxMeasurePolicy(): MeasurePolicy =
    MeasurePolicy { measurables, constraints ->
        val placeables = measurables.map { measurable ->
            measurable.measure(constraints)
        }
        layout(
            constraints.maxWidth,
```

```
            constraints.maxHeight
    ) {
        var yPos = 0
        var xPos = 0
        var maxY = 0
        placeables.forEach { placeable ->
            if (xPos + placeable.width >
                constraints.maxWidth
            ) {
                xPos = 0
                yPos += maxY
                maxY = 0
            }
            placeable.placeRelative(
                x = xPos,
                y = yPos
            )
            xPos += placeable.width
            if (maxY < placeable.height) {
                maxY = placeable.height
            }
        }
    }
}
```

MeasurePolicy implementations must provide implementations of MeasureScope.
measure(). This function returns an instance of the MeasureResult interface.
You do not need to implement this on your own. Instead, you must invoke layout().
This function belongs to MeasureScope.

We pass the measured size of the layout and a placementBlock, which is an extension
function of Placeable.PlacementScope. This means that you can invoke functions
such as placeRelative() to position a child in its parent's coordinate system.

A measure policy receives the content, or children, as `List<Measurable>`. As you know from the *Understanding the single measure pass* section, children must be measured exactly once before they are positioned. We can do this by creating a map of `placeables`, invoking `measure()` on each `measurable`. My example doesn't constrain child views further, instead measuring them with the given constraints.

`placementBlock` iterates over the `placeables` map, calculating the location of a placeable by increasing `xPos` and `yPos` along the way. Before invoking `placeRelative()`, the algorithm checks if a placeable completely fits into the current row. If this is not the case, `yPos` will be increased and `xPos` will be reset to `0`. How much `yPos` will be increased depends on the maximum height of all the placeables in the current row. This value is stored in `maxY`.

As you have seen, implementing simple custom layouts is straightforward. Advanced topics such as alignment lines (which help with/are needed for X...) are beyond the scope of this book. You can find more information about them at `https://developer.android.com/jetpack/compose/layouts/alignment-lines`.

Summary

This chapter explored the predefined layouts of `Row()`, `Column()`, and `Box()`. You learned how to combine them to create beautiful UIs. You were also introduced to `ConstraintLayout`, which places composables that are relative to others on the screen and flattens the UI element hierarchy.

The second main section explored why the layout system in Jetpack Compose is more performant than the traditional View-based approach. We looked at some of the internals of the Compose runtime, which prepared us for the final main section of this chapter, *Creating custom layouts*, where you learned how to create a custom layout and thus gain precise control over the rendering of its children.

The next chapter, *Managing the State of Your Composable Functions*, will deepen your knowledge of state. We will examine the difference between stateless and stateful composable functions. Also, we will look at advanced use cases such as surviving configuration changes.

5

Managing the State of Your Composable Functions

In *Chapter 4*, *Laying Out UI Elements*, I showed you how to set the red, green, and blue portions of a color by dragging sliders. We used **state** to share these values among composable functions. Quite a few other sample apps of the previous chapters dealt with state, too. In fact, reacting to state changes is critical to how modern mobile apps work.

So far, I have described state as data that can change over time. You learned about a few important functions, for example, `remember { }` and `mutableStateOf()`. I also briefly touched on a concept called **state hoisting**.

This chapter builds on these foundations. For example, you will understand the difference between stateless and stateful composables, and when to choose which. Also, I will show you how events should flow in a well-behaving Compose app.

The main sections of this chapter are the following:

- Understanding stateful and stateless composable functions
- Hoisting state and passing events
- Surviving configuration changes

We will start by exploring the differences between stateful and stateless composable functions. You will learn their typical use cases and understand why you should try to keep your composables stateless. Hoisting state is a tool to achieve that; we will cover this important topic in the second main section. Also, I will show you that you can make your composable functions reusable by passing logic as parameters, rather than implementing it inside the composable.

Finally, the *Surviving configuration changes* section will explore the integration of a Compose UI hierarchy in activities, concerning how to retain user input. If the user changes from portrait to landscape mode (or vice versa), activities are destroyed and recreated. Of course, input should not be lost. We look at several ways that a Compose app can achieve this.

Technical requirements

This chapter includes three sample apps. Please refer to the *Technical requirements* section in *Chapter 1*, *Building Your First Compose App*, for information about how to install and set up Android Studio, and how to get them. StateDemo contains all examples from the *Understanding stateful and stateless composable functions* section. The *Hoisting state and passing events* section discusses the FlowOfEventsDemo sample. Finally, ViewModelDemo belongs to the *Surviving configuration changes* section.

All the code files for this chapter can be found on GitHub at https://github.com/PacktPublishing/Android-UI-Development-with-Jetpack-Compose/tree/main/chapter_05.

Understanding stateful and stateless composable functions

In this section, I will show you the difference between stateful and stateless composable functions. To understand why this is important, let's first focus on the **state** term. In previous chapters, I described state as *data that can change over time*. Where the data is held (an SQLite database, a file, or a value inside an object) does not matter. What is important is that the UI must always show the current data. Therefore, if a value changes, the UI must be notified. To achieve this, we use **observable** types. This is not specific to Jetpack Compose, but a common pattern in many frameworks, programming languages, and platforms. For example, Kotlin supports observables through property delegates:

```
var counter by observable(-1) { _, oldValue, newValue ->
  println("$oldValue -> $newValue")
```

```
}
for (i in 0..3) counter = i
```

observable() returns a delegate for a property that can be read and written to. In the previous code snippet, the initial value is set to -1. The property calls a specified function when its value is changed (counter = i). My example prints the old and new values. In an imperative UI framework, state changes require modifying the component tree. Such code could be put in the callback function. Fortunately, Jetpack Compose doesn't require this, because state changes automatically trigger a recomposition of the relevant UI elements. Let's see how this works.

The androidx.compose.runtime.State base interface defines a value holder, an object that stores a value of a particular type in a property named value. If this property is read during the execution of a composable function, the composable will be recomposed whenever value changes, because internally the current RecomposeScope interface will be subscribed to changes of that value. Please note that to be able to change the value, state must be an implementation of MutableState; unlike its immediate predecessor (State), this interface defines value using var instead of val.

The easiest way to create State instances is to invoke mutableStateOf(). This function returns a new MutableState instance, initialized with the value that was passed in. The next section explains how to use mutableStateOf() to create a stateful composable function.

Using state in a composable function

A composable function is said to be **stateful** if it maintains (remembers) some value. We achieve this by invoking remember {}. Let's take a look:

```
@Composable
@Preview
fun SimpleStateDemo1() {
    val num = remember { mutableStateOf(Random.nextInt(0,
        10)) }
    Text(text = num.value.toString())
}
```

`SimpleStateDemo1()` creates a mutable state holding a random integer. By invoking `remember {}`, we save the state, and in using =, we assign it to num. We get the random number through `num.value`. Please note that although we defined num with the `val` keyword, we could change the value with `num.value = ...`, because num holds the reference to a mutable value holder (whose `value` property is writeable). Think of it as modifying an item in a list, not changing to another list. We can slightly alter the code, as shown in the following snippet. Can you spot the difference?

```
@Composable
@Preview
fun SimpleStateDemo2() {
    val num by remember { mutableStateOf(Random.nextInt(0,
        10)) }
    Text(text = num.toString())
}
```

`SimpleStateDemo2()` creates a mutable state holding a random integer number, too. Using by, we do not assign the state itself to num but the value it stores (the random number). This spares us from using `.value`, which makes the code a little shorter and hopefully more understandable. However, if we want to change num, we must change `val` to `var`. Otherwise, we see a `Val cannot be reassigned` error message.

You may be wondering what `remember {}` does under the hood. Let's peek into its code and find out:

```
     Remember the value produced by calculation. calculation will only be evaluated during the composition.
     Recomposition will always return the value produced by composition.
23   @Composable
24   inline fun <T> remember(calculation: @DisallowComposableCalls () -> T): T =
25       currentComposer.cache( invalid: false, calculation)
26
```

Figure 5.1 – The source code of remember {}

The read-only, top-level `currentComposer` property belongs to the `androidx.compose.runtime` package. It references an instance of `Composer`. This interface is targeted by the Compose Kotlin compiler plugin and used by code generation helpers. You should not call it directly, because the runtime assumes that calls are generated by the compiler and therefore do not contain much validation logic. `Cache()` is an extension function of `Composer`. It stores a value in the composition data of a composition. So, `remember {}` creates internal state. Therefore, composable functions that contain `remember {}` are stateful.

`calculation` represents a lambda expression that creates the value to be remembered. It is evaluated only once, during the composition. Subsequent calls to `remember {}` (during recompositions) always return this value. The expression is not evaluated again. But what if we need to reevaluate the calculation, that is, remember a new value? After all, isn't state data that can change over time? Here's how you can do this:

```
@Composable
@Preview
fun RememberWithKeyDemo() {
    var key by remember { mutableStateOf(false) }
    val date by remember(key) { mutableStateOf(Date()) }
    Column(horizontalAlignment =
            Alignment.CenterHorizontally) {
        Text(date.toString())
        Button(onClick = { key = !key }) {
            Text(text = stringResource(id = R.string.click))
        }
    }
}
```

The preview of `RememberWithKeyDemo()` is shown in *Figure 5.2*:

Figure 5.2 – Preview of RememberWithKeyDemo()

`RememberWithKeyDemo()` emits `Column()` with two horizontally centered children:

- `Text()` shows the string representation of a remembered `Date` instance.
- `Button()` toggles a Boolean value (`key`).

Have you noticed that I pass `key` to `remember { mutableStateOf(Date()) }`? Here's what happens – when `remember {}` is invoked for the first time, the result of the calculation (`mutableStateOf(Date())`) is remembered and returned. During recompositions, the calculation is not reevaluated unless `key` is *not* equal to the previous composition. In this case, a new value is calculated, remembered, and returned.

> **Tip**
>
> You can pass any number of keys to remember { }. If one of them has changed since the previous composition, the calculation is reevaluated, and the new value is remembered and returned.

Passing keys to remember { } allows you to change remembered values. Please keep in mind, though, that this makes the composable function less predictable. Therefore, you should consider whether such logic needs to be composable or whether you could pass all state to it.

In the next section, we turn to stateless composables.

Writing stateless composable functions

remember { } makes a composable function stateful. A stateless composable, on the other hand, doesn't hold any state. Here's an example:

```
@Composable
@Preview
fun SimpleStatelessComposable1() {
  Text(text = "Hello Compose")
}
```

SimpleStatelessComposable1() doesn't receive parameters and it always calls Text() with the same parameters. Clearly, it doesn't hold any state. But how about the following one?

```
@Composable
fun SimpleStatelessComposable2(text: State<String>) {
  Text(text = text.value)
}
```

While it receives state through the text parameter, it doesn't store it, and it doesn't remember other state. Consequently, SimpleStatelessComposable2() is stateless, too. It behaves the same way when called with the same argument multiple times. Such functions are said to be **idempotent**. This makes SimpleStatelessComposable2() a good blueprint for your own composable functions. They should be as follows:

- **Fast**: Your composable must not do heavy (that is, time-consuming) computations. Never invoke a web service or do any other I/O. Data that is used by a composable should be passed to it.

- **Free of side-effects**: Do not modify global properties or produce unintended observable effects (modifying state that has been passed to a composable is certainly intentional).

- **Idempotent**: Do not use `remember { }`, do not access global properties, and do not call unpredictable code. For example, `SimpleStateDemo1()` and `SimpleStateDemo2()` use `Random.nextInt()`, which, by definition, is (practically) not predictable.

Such composable functions are both easy to reuse and test because they don't rely on anything that isn't passed in as parameters.

When developing reusable composables, you may want to expose both a stateful and a stateless version. Let's see how this looks:

```
@Composable
fun TextFieldDemo(state: MutableState<TextFieldValue>) {
  TextField(
    value = state.value,
    onValueChange = {
      state.value = it
    },
    placeholder = { Text("Hello") },
    modifier = Modifier.fillMaxWidth()
  )
}
```

This version is stateless because it receives state and does not remember anything. Stateless versions are necessary for callers that need to control the state or hoist it themselves:

```
@Composable
@Preview
fun TextFieldDemo() {
  val state = remember { mutableStateOf(TextFieldValue("")) }
  TextFieldDemo(state)
}
```

This version is stateful because it remembers the state it creates. Stateful versions are convenient for callers that don't care about the state.

To conclude, try to make your composables stateless by not relying on `remember { }` or other functions that remember state (for example, `rememberLazyListState()` or `rememberSaveable()`). Instead, pass state to the composable. You will see more use cases in the next section.

Hoisting state and passing events

So, state is any value that can change over time. As Jetpack Compose is a declarative UI framework, the only way to update a composable is to call it with new arguments. This happens automatically when state a composable is using changes. State hoisting is a pattern of moving state up to make a composable stateless.

Besides making a composable more easily reusable and testable, moving state up is necessary to use it in more than one composable function. You have already seen this in quite a few of my sample apps. For example, in the *Composing and recomposing the UI* section of *Chapter 3*, *Exploring the Key Principles of Compose*, we used three sliders to create and display a color.

While state controls the visual representation of a composable function (that is, how it looks on screen), **events** notify a part of a program that something has happened. Let's focus a little more on this. My sample `FlowOfEventsDemo` app is a simple temperature converter. The user enters a value, specifies whether it represents degrees Celsius or Fahrenheit, and then hits the **Convert** button:

Figure 5.3 – Sample FlowOfEventsDemo app

The UI consists of `Column()` with four children: a text input field, a group of radio buttons with text, a button, and some result text. Let's look at the text input field first:

```
@Composable
fun TemperatureTextField(
    temperature: MutableState<String>,
```

```
  modifier: Modifier = Modifier,
  callback: () -> Unit
) {
  TextField(
    value = temperature.value,
    onValueChange = {
      temperature.value = it
    },
    ...
    modifier = modifier,
    keyboardActions = KeyboardActions(onAny = {
      callback()
    }),
    keyboardOptions = KeyboardOptions(
      keyboardType = KeyboardType.Number,
      imeAction = ImeAction.Done
    ),
    singleLine = true
  )
}
```

It receives `MutableState<String>`, to which it pushes changes to the text in
`onValueChange { }`. The virtual keyboard is configured to show a *Done* button. If it is
invoked, code passed to the composable through `callback` is executed. As you will see
a little later, that same code will run if the user clicks on the *Convert* button.

In the next section, I'll show you how to create radio buttons and put them in groups so
that only one button is selected at a time. The section also covers the button and the result
text, which you can see in *Fig. 5.3.*

Creating radio button groups

The app converts between degrees Celsius and Fahrenheit. Therefore, the user must
choose the target scale. Such selections can be implemented easily in Jetpack Compose
using `androidx.compose.material.RadioButton()`. This composable doesn't
show some descriptive text, but it is easy to add some. Here's how:

```
@Composable
fun TemperatureRadioButton(
```

```
    selected: Boolean,
    resId: Int,
    onClick: (Int) -> Unit,
    modifier: Modifier = Modifier
) {
    Row(
        verticalAlignment = Alignment.CenterVertically,
        modifier = modifier
    ) {
        RadioButton(
            selected = selected,
            onClick = {
                onClick(resId)
            }
        )
        Text(
            text = stringResource(resId),
            modifier = Modifier
                .padding(start = 8.dp)
        )
    }
}
```

RadioButton() and Text() are simply added to Row() and vertically centered.
TemperatureRadioButton() receives a lambda expression with the onClick
parameter. That code is executed when the radio button is clicked. My implementation
passes the resId parameter to the lambda expression, which will be used to determine
the button in a group. Here's how:

```
@Composable
fun TemperatureScaleButtonGroup(
    selected: MutableState<Int>,
    modifier: Modifier = Modifier
) {
    val sel = selected.value
    val onClick = { resId: Int -> selected.value = resId }
    Row(modifier = modifier) {
        TemperatureRadioButton(
```

```
        selected = sel == R.string.celsius,
        resId = R.string.celsius,
        onClick = onClick
    )
    TemperatureRadioButton(
        selected = sel == R.string.fahrenheit,
        resId = R.string.fahrenheit,
        onClick = onClick,
        modifier = Modifier.padding(start = 16.dp)
    )
    }
}
```

Two `TemperatureRadioButton()` are put in a `Row()`. The first one is configured to represent degrees Celsius, the second one degrees Fahrenheit. Both receive the same `onClick` lambda. It sets the `resId` parameter it received from `TemperatureRadioButton()` as the new value of the `selected` parameter, a mutable state. So, what is happening here? Clicks on a radio button are not handled inside `TemperatureRadioButton()` but passed to the parent, `TemperatureScaleButtonGroup()`. The event, a button click, is said to **bubble up**. This way, the parent can orchestrate its children and notify its parent. In my example, this means changing some state.

Next, let's see what happens when the user clicks the **Convert** button. This happens inside `FlowOfEventsDemo()`. Here's the overall structure of this composable function:

```
@Composable
@Preview
fun FlowOfEventsDemo() {
    ...
    val calc = {
        val temp = temperature.value.toFloat()
        convertedTemperature = if (scale.value ==
                                    R.string.celsius)
            (temp * 1.8F) + 32F
        else
            (temp - 32F) / 1.8F
    }
    val result = remember(convertedTemperature) {
```

```
    if (convertedTemperature.isNaN())
        ""
    else
        "${convertedTemperature}${
            if (scale.value == R.string.celsius)
                strFahrenheit
            else strCelsius
        }"
}
val enabled = temperature.value.isNotBlank()
Column( ... ) {
    TemperatureTextField(
        temperature = temperature,
        modifier = Modifier.padding(bottom = 16.dp),
        callback = calc
    )
    TemperatureScaleButtonGroup(
        selected = scale,
        modifier = Modifier.padding(bottom = 16.dp)
    )
    Button(
        onClick = calc,
        enabled = enabled
    ) {
        Text( ... )
    }
    if (result.isNotEmpty()) {
        Text(text = result, …
        )
    }
  }
}
```

The conversion logic is assigned to a read-only variable called calc. It is passed to TemperatureTextField() and Button(). Passing the code that is going to be executed in response to an event to a composable function rather than hard coding it inside makes the composable more easily reusable and testable.

The text that is displayed after conversion is remembered and assigned to `result`. It is re-evaluated when `convertedTemperature` changes. This happens inside the `calc` lambda expression. Please note that I need to pass a key to `remember {}`; otherwise, the result would be changed also if the user picks another scale.

In the next section, we will look at how state can be persisted. To be more precise, we turn to configuration changes. If the user rotates a device, the UI should not be reset. Unfortunately, this is what happens with all sample apps I have shown you so far. It's time to fix this.

Surviving configuration changes

Please recall that our definition of state as data that may change over time is quite broad. For example, we do not specify where the data is stored. If it resides in a database, a file, or some backend in the cloud, the app should include a dedicated persistence layer. However, until Google introduced the Android Architecture Components back in 2017, there had been practically no guidance for developers on how to structure their apps. Consequently, persistence code, UI logic, and domain logic were often crammed into one activity. Such code was difficult to maintain and often prone to errors. To make matters a little more complicated, there are situations when an activity is destroyed and recreated shortly after. For example, this happens when a user rotates a device. Certainly, data should then be remembered.

The `Activity` class has a few methods to handle this. For example, `onSaveInstanceState()` is invoked when the activity is (temporarily) destroyed. Its counterpart `onRestoreInstanceState()` method is called only when such an instance state has been saved before. Both methods receive an instance of `Bundle`, which has getters and setters for various data types. However, the concept of instance state has been designed for the traditional view system. Most activities held references to UI elements and therefore could be accessed easily inside `onSaveInstanceState()` and `onRestoreInstanceState()`.

Composables, on the other hand, are usually implemented as top-level functions. So, how can their state be set or queried from inside an activity? To temporarily save state in a Compose app, you can use `rememberSaveable {}`. This composable function remembers the value produced by a factory function. It behaves similarly to `remember {}`. The stored value will survive the activity or process recreation. Internally, the `savedInstanceState` mechanism is used. The sample `ViewModelDemo` app shows how to use `rememberSaveable {}`. Here's what the main activity looks like:

```
class ViewModelDemoActivity : ComponentActivity() {
    override fun onCreate(savedInstanceState: Bundle?) {
```

```
    super.onCreate(savedInstanceState)
    setContent {
      ViewModelDemo()
    }
  }
}
```

We don't need to override onSaveInstanceState() to temporarily save our state used with composables:

```
@Composable
@Preview
fun ViewModelDemo() {
  ...
  val state1 = remember {
    mutableStateOf("Hello #1")
  }
  val state2 = rememberSaveable {
    mutableStateOf("Hello #2")
  }
  ...
  state3.value?.let {
    Column(modifier = Modifier.fillMaxWidth()) {
      MyTextField(state1) { state1.value = it }
      MyTextField(state2) { state2.value = it }
      ...
    }
  }
}
```

The app shows three text input fields that receive their values from states assigned to state1, state2, and state3. For now, we will focus on the first two. state3 will be the subject of the *Using ViewModel* section. state1 invokes remember {}, whereas state2 uses rememberSaveable {}. If you ran ViewModelDemo, changed the content of the text input fields, and rotated the device, the first one would be reset to the original text, whereas the second one would keep your changes.

`MyTextField` is a very simple composable. It looks like this:

```
@Composable
fun MyTextField(
  value: State<String?>,
  onValueChange: (String) -> Unit
) {
  value.value?.let {
    TextField(
      value = it,
      onValueChange = onValueChange,
      modifier = Modifier.fillMaxWidth()
    )
  }
}
```

Have you noticed that `value` is of `State<String?>`? Why would I need a value holder whose value can be `null`, and therefore need to check with `value.value?.let {}` that it isn't? We will be reusing the composable in the following section, and you will find the answer to this question there. Please note, though, that for both `state1` and `state2`, this would not have been necessary.

Using ViewModel

While temporarily storing state with `rememberSaveable {}` works great, an app still must get data that is persisted for a longer time (for example, in a database or file) and make it available as state that can be used in composables. The Android Architecture Components include `ViewModel` and `LiveData`. Both can be used seamlessly with Jetpack Compose.

First, you need to add a few implementation dependencies to the module-level `build.gradle` file:

```
implementation "androidx.compose.runtime:runtime-
  livedata:$compose_version"
implementation 'androidx.lifecycle:lifecycle-runtime-
  ktx:2.4.0'
implementation 'androidx.lifecycle:lifecycle-viewmodel-
  compose:2.4.0'
```

The next step is to define a `ViewModel` class. It extends `androidx.lifecycle.ViewModel`. A `ViewModel` class stores and manages UI-related data in a lifecycle-conscious way. This means that data will survive configuration changes, such as screen rotations. `MyViewModel` exposes one property called `text` and a method named `setText()` to set it:

```
class MyViewModel : ViewModel() {

    private val _text: MutableLiveData<String> =
        MutableLiveData<String>("Hello #3")

    val text: LiveData<String>
        get() = _text

    fun setText(value: String) {
        _text.value = value
    }
}
```

My example shows a `ViewModel` class using `LiveData`. Depending on the architecture of an app, you can utilize other mechanisms for working with observable data. Going into more detail is, however, beyond the scope of this book. You can find additional information in *Guide to app architecture* at `https://developer.android.com/jetpack/guide`.

To access the `ViewModel` class from inside a composable function, we invoke the composable `viewModel()`. It belongs to the `androidx.lifecycle.viewmodel.compose` package:

```
val viewModel: MyViewModel = viewModel()
```

`LiveData` is made available as state like this:

```
val state3 = viewModel.text.observeAsState()
```

Let's take a quick look at its source code:

```
Starts observing this LiveData and represents its values via State. Every time there would be new value
posted into the LiveData the returned State will be updated causing recomposition of every State.value
usage.

The inner observer will automatically be removed when this composable disposes or the current
LifecycleOwner moves to the Lifecycle.State.DESTROYED state.

Samples: androidx.compose.runtime.livedata.samples.LiveDataSample
            // Unresolved

40   @Composable
41   fun <T> LiveData<T>.observeAsState(): State<T?> = observeAsState(value)
```

Figure 5.4 – Source code of the observeAsState() extension function

observeAsState() is an extension function of LiveData. It passes the value property of its LiveData instance to a variant of observeAsState() that takes parameters. Have you noticed that the return type is State<T?>? That is why I defined MyTextField() in the previous section to receive State<String?>. To be able to use State<String> as with remember {} and rememberSaveable {}, we would need to define state3 like this:

```
val state3 =
    viewModel.text.observeAsState(viewModel.text.value) as
    State<String>
```

In my opinion, this is less favorable than using State<String?> because we use an unchecked cast.

To reflect changes in state in the ViewModel class, we need code like this:

```
MyTextField(state3) {
    viewModel.setText(it)
}
```

Unlike using MutableState, we must explicitly invoke the setText() method of MyViewModel and pass the changed text.

To conclude, rememberSaveable {} is simple and easy to use. For more complex scenarios than presented in this chapter, you can provide androidx.compose.runtime.saveable.Saver implementations, which make your data objects simpler and convert them to something saveable. Bigger apps should use ViewModel classes, as recommended for quite a while now by Google. The combination of ViewModel and LiveData classes can be integrated nicely into composable apps using observerAsState().

Summary

This chapter aimed to give a more detailed look at state in Compose apps. We started by exploring the differences between stateful and stateless composable functions. You learned their typical use cases and why you should try to keep your composables stateless. Hoisting state is a tool to achieve that. We covered this important topic in the second main section. I also showed you that you can make your composable functions more reusable by passing logic as parameters, rather than implementing it inside the composable. The previous section explored the integration of a Compose UI hierarchy in activities concerning how to retain user input. We looked at the differences between `remember {}` and `rememberSaveable {}`, and I gave you a glimpse of how bigger Compose apps can benefit from `ViewModel` classes.

Chapters 1 to 5 introduced you to various aspects of Jetpack Compose, such as composable functions, state, and layout. *Chapter 6, Putting Pieces Together*, focuses on one app, providing you with a bigger picture of how these pieces work together to form a real-world app. We will implement a simple unit converter app, focusing on app architecture and UI, including theming and navigation.

6
Putting Pieces Together

The previous chapters explored various aspects of Jetpack Compose. For example, *Chapter 2, Understanding the Declarative Paradigm*, compared the traditional View system to composable functions and explained the benefits of the declarative approach. *Chapter 4, Laying Out UI Elements*, gave you a solid understanding of some built-in layout composables such as Box(), Row(), and Column(). In *Chapter 5, Managing the State of Your Composable Functions*, we looked at state and learned about the important role it plays in a Compose app.

Now, it's time to see how these key elements work together in a real-world app. In this chapter, you will learn how Compose apps can be themed. We will also look at Scaffold(), an integrational UI element that picks up quite a few concepts that were originally related to activities, such as toolbars and menus, and we will learn how to add screen-based navigation.

In this chapter, we will cover the following topics:

- Styling a Compose app
- Integrating toolbars and menus
- Adding navigation

We will start by setting up a custom theme for a Compose app. You can define quite a few colors, shapes, and text styles that the built-in Material composables will use when drawing themselves. I will also show you what to keep in mind when you're adding additional Jetpack components that rely on app themes, such as *Jetpack Core Splashscreen*.

The following section, *Integrating toolbars and menus*, will introduce you to app bars and the options menu. You will also learn how to create snack bars.

In the final main section, *Adding navigation*, I will show you how to structure your app into screens. We will use the Compose version of *Jetpack Navigation* to navigate between them.

Technical requirements

This chapter includes one sample app, `ComposeUnitConverter`, as shown in the following screenshot:

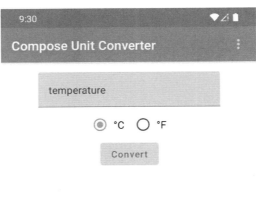

Figure 6.1 – The ComposeUnitConverter app

Please refer to the *Technical requirements* section of *Chapter 1, Building Your First Compose App,* for information about how to install and set up Android Studio, as well as how to get the repository that accompanies this book.

All the code files for this chapter can be found on GitHub at `https://github.com/PacktPublishing/Android-UI-Development-with-Jetpack-Compose/tree/main/chapter_06`.

Styling a Compose app

Most of your Compose UI will likely use the built-in composable functions from the `androidx.compose.material` package. They implement the design language known as **Material Design** and its successor, **Material You** (which was introduced with Android 12). Material You is the native design language on Android, though it will also be available on other platforms. It expands on the ideas of a pen, paper, and cards, and makes heavy use of grid-based layouts, responsive animations, and transitions, as well as padding and depth effects. Material You advocates larger buttons and rounded corners. Custom color themes can be generated from the user's wallpaper.

Defining colors, shapes, and text styles

While apps should certainly honor both system and user preferences regarding visual appearance, you may want to add colors, shapes, or text styles that reflect your brand or corporate identity. So, how can you modify the look of the built-in Material composable functions?

The main entry point to Material Theming is `MaterialTheme()`. This composable may receive custom colors, shapes, and text styles. If a value is not set, a corresponding default (`MaterialTheme.colors`, `MaterialTheme.typography`, or `MaterialTheme.shapes`) is used. The following theme sets custom colors but leaves the text styles and shapes as their defaults:

```
@Composable
fun ComposeUnitConverterTheme(
    darkTheme: Boolean = isSystemInDarkTheme(),
    content: @Composable () -> Unit
) {
    val colors = if (darkTheme) {
        DarkColorPalette
    } else {
        LightColorPalette
    }
    MaterialTheme(
        colors = colors,
        content = content
    )
}
```

The isSystemInDarkTheme() composable detects if the device is currently using a dark theme. Your app should use colors that suit this configuration. My example has two palettes, DarkColorPalette and LightColorPalette. Here's how the latter one is defined:

```
private val LightColorPalette = lightColors(
  primary = AndroidGreen,
  primaryVariant = AndroidGreenDark,
  secondary = Orange,
  secondaryVariant = OrangeDark
)
```

lightColors() is a top-level function inside the androidx.compose.material package. It provides a complete color definition for the Material color specification. You can find more information about this at https://material.io/design/color/the-color-system.html#color-theme-creation. LightColorPalette overrides the default values for primary, primaryVariant, secondary, and secondaryVariant. All the others (there are, for example, background, surface, and onPrimary) remain unchanged.

primary will be displayed most frequently across your app's screens and components. With secondary, you can accent and distinguish your app. It is, for example, used for radio buttons. The checked thumb color of switches is secondaryVariant, whereas the unchecked thumb color is taken from surface.

> **Tip**
> Material composables typically receive their default colors from composable functions called colors(), which belong to their accompanying ...Defaults objects. For example, Switch() invokes SwitchDefaults.colors() if no color parameter is passed to Switch(). By looking at these colors() functions, you can find out which color attribute you should set in your theme.

You may be wondering how I defined, for example, AndroidGreen. The simplest way to achieve this is like this:

```
val AndroidGreen = Color(0xFF3DDC84)
```

This works great if your app does not require other libraries or components that rely on the traditional Android theming system. We will turn to such scenarios in the *Using resource-based themes* section.

Besides colors, `MaterialTheme()` allows you to provide alternative shapes. Shapes direct attention and communicate state. Material composables are grouped into shape categories based on their size:

- Small (buttons, snack bars, tooltips, and more)
- Medium (cards, dialog, menus, and more)
- Large (sheets and drawers, and more)

To pass an alternative set of shapes to `MaterialTheme()`, you must instantiate `androidx.compose.material.Shapes` and provide implementations of the `androidx.compose.foundation.shape.CornerBasedShape` abstract class for the categories you want to modify (`small`, `medium`, and `large`). `AbsoluteCutCornerShape`, `CutCornerShape`, `AbsoluteRoundedCornerShape`, and `RoundedCornerShape` are direct subclasses of `CornerBasedShape`.

The following screenshot shows a button with cut corners. While this makes the button look less familiar, it gives your app a distinctive look. You should, however, ensure that you want to add this:

Figure 6.2 – A button with cut corners

To achieve this, just add the following line when invoking `MaterialTheme()`:

```
shapes = Shapes(small = CutCornerShape(8.dp)),
```

You can find more information about applying shapes to UIs at `https://material.io/design/shape/applying-shape-to-ui.html#shape-scheme`.

To alter the text styles that are used by Material composable functions, you need to pass an instance of `androidx.compose.material.Typography` to `MaterialTheme()`. `Typography` receives quite a few parameters, such as `h1`, `subtitle1`, `body1`, `button`, and `caption`. All of these are instances of `androidx.compose.ui.text.TextStyle`. If you do not pass a value for a parameter, a default is used.

The following code block increases the text size of buttons:

```
typography = Typography(button = TextStyle(fontSize =
                                      24.sp)),
```

If you add this line to the invocation of `MaterialTheme()`, the text of all the buttons using your theme will be 24 scale-independent pixels tall. But how do you set the theme? To make sure that your complete Compose UI uses it, you should invoke your theme as early as possible:

```
class ComposeUnitConverterActivity : ComponentActivity() {
  override fun onCreate(savedInstanceState: Bundle?) {
    super.onCreate(savedInstanceState)
    val factory = …
    setContent {
      ComposeUnitConverter(factory)
    }
  }
}
```

In my example, `ComposeUnitConverter()` is the root of the app's composable UI hierarchy since it is invoked inside `setContent {}`:

```
@Composable
fun ComposeUnitConverter(factory: ViewModelFactory) {
  …
  ComposeUnitConverterTheme {
    Scaffold( ...
```

`ComposeUnitConverter()` immediately delegates to `ComposeUnitConverterTheme {}`, which receives the remaining UI as its content. `Scaffold()` is a skeleton for real-world Compose UIs. We will be taking a closer look at this in the *Integrating toolbars and menus* section.

If you need to style parts of your app differently, you can nest themes by overriding your parent theme (*Figure 6.3*). Let's see how this works:

```
@Composable
@Preview
fun MaterialThemeDemo() {
  MaterialTheme(
    typography = Typography(
      h1 = TextStyle(color = Color.Red)
    )
  ) {
```

```
Row {
    Text(
        text"= "He"lo",
        style = MaterialTheme.typography.h1
    )
    Spacer(modifier = Modifier.width(2.dp))
    MaterialTheme(
        typography = Typography(
            h1 = TextStyle(color = Color.Blue)
        )
    ) {
        Text(
            text"= "Comp"se",
            style = MaterialTheme.typography.h1
        )
    }
  }
}
```

In the preceding code snippet, the base theme configures any text that is styled as h1 so that it appears in red. The second Text() uses a nested theme that styles h1 to appear in blue. So, it overrides the parent theme:

Figure 6.3 – Nesting themes

> **Please Note**
> All the parts of your app must have a consistent look. Consequently, you should use nested themes carefully.

In the next section, we will continue exploring styles and themes. We will look at how themes are set in the manifest file, as well as how libraries may influence the way you define your Compose theme.

Using resource-based themes

App styling or theming has been present on Android since API level 1. It is based on resource files. Conceptually, there is a distinction between styles and themes. A **style** is a collection of attributes that specify the appearance (for example, font color, font size, or background color) of a single View. Consequently, styles do not matter for composable functions. A **theme** is also a collection of attributes, but it's applied to an entire app, activity, or View hierarchy. Many elements of a Compose app are provided by Material composables; for them, a resource-based theme does not matter either. However, themes can apply styles to non-View elements, such as the status bar and window background. This may be relevant for a Compose app.

Styles and themes are declared in XML files inside the `res/values` directory and are typically named `styles.xml` and `themes.xml`, depending on the content. A theme is applied to the application or activity inside the manifest file with the `android:theme` attribute of the `<application />` or `<activity />` tag. If none of them receives a theme, `ComposeUnitConverter` will look as follows:

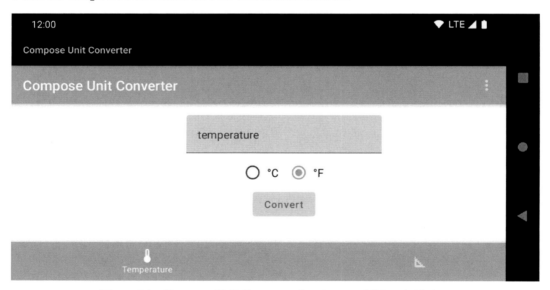

Figure 6.4 – Compose Unit Converter showing an additional title bar

To avoid the unwanted additional title bar, Compose apps must configure a theme without action bars, such as `Theme.AppCompat.DayNight.NoActionBar`, using `android:the"e="@styl"/..."` for `<application />` or `<activity />`. This way, `ComposeUnitConverter` looks like *Figure 6.1*. Have you noticed that the status bar has a dark gray background?

When `Theme.AppCompat.DayNight` is used, the status bar receives its background color from the `colorPrimaryDark` theme attribute (or `android:statusBarColor` since API level 21). If no value is specified, a default is used. Therefore, to make sure that the status bar is shown in a color that fits the remaining UI elements, you must add a file named `themes.xml` to `res/values`:

```
<resources>
    <style name="Theme.ComposeUnitConverter"
            parent="Theme.AppCompat.DayNight.NoActionBar">
        <item
        name="colorPrimaryDark">@color/android_green_dark
        </item>
    </style>
</resources>
```

In the manifest file, the value of `android:theme` must then be changed to `@style/Theme.ComposeUnitConverter`. `@color/android_green_dark` represents the color. Instead of this expression, you could also pass the value directly; for example, `#FF20B261`. It is, however, best practice to store it in a file named `colors.xml` inside `res/values`:

```
<resources>
    <color name="android_green_dark">#FF20B261</color>
    <color name="orange_dark">#FFCC8400</color>
</resources>
```

This way, you can assign a different value for the Dark theme. The following version of `themes.xml` should be put in `res/values-night`:

```
<resources>
    <style name="Theme.ComposeUnitConverter"
            parent="Theme.AppCompat.DayNight.NoActionBar">
        <item name="colorPrimaryDark">@color/orange_dark</item>
    </style>
</resources>
```

The status bar now has a background color that fits the remaining UI elements. However, we need to define colors in two places: `colors.xml` and the Compose theme. Fortunately, this is rather easy to fix. Usually, we pass a literal, like this:

```
val AndroidGreenDark = Color(0xFF20B261)
```

Instead of doing this, we should obtain the value from the resources. The
colorResource() composable function belongs to the androidx.compose.
ui.res package. It returns the color associated with a resource that's identified by an ID.

The following palette does not specify a secondary color:

```
private val LightColorPalette = lightColors(
  primary = AndroidGreen,
  primaryVariant = AndroidGreenDark,
  secondaryVariant = OrangeDark
)
```

Adding a color using colorResource() works as follows:

```
@Composable
fun ComposeUnitConverterTheme(
  darkTheme: Boolean = isSystemInDarkTheme(),
  content: @Composable () -> Unit
) {
  val colors = if (darkTheme) {
    DarkColorPalette
  } else {
    LightColorPalette.copy(secondary = colorResource(
      id = R.color.orange_dark))
  }
  MaterialTheme(
    colors = colors,
    ...
```

You saw most of this in the *Defining colors, shapes, and text styles* section. The important
difference is that I created a modified version of LightColorPalette (with a secondary
color) using copy(), which is then passed to MaterialTheme(). If you store all the
colors inside colors.xml, you should create your palettes completely inside your
theme composable.

As you have seen, you may need to provide some values for resource-based themes, depending on how heavily you want to brand your app. Additionally, certain non-Compose Jetpack libraries use themes too, such as *Jetpack Core Splashscreen*. This component makes the advanced splash screen features of Android 12 available on older platforms. The images and colors of the splash screen are configured through theme attributes. The library requires that the theme of the starting activity has `Theme.SplashScreen` as its parent. Additionally, the theme must provide the `postSplashScreenTheme` attribute, which refers to the theme to use once the splash screen has been dismissed. You can find more information about splash screens on Android at `https://developer.android.com/guide/topics/ui/splash-screen`.

> **Tip**
>
> To ensure consistent use of colors, the `colors.xml` file should be the single point of truth in your app, if more than one component relies on resource-based themes.

This concludes our look at Compose themes. In the next section, we will turn to an important integrational UI element called **Scaffold**. `Scaffold()` acts as a frame for your content, providing support for top and bottom bars, navigation, and actions.

Integrating toolbars and menus

Early Android versions did not know about action or app bars. They were introduced with API level 11 (Honeycomb). The options menu, on the other hand, has been around since the beginning but was opened by pressing a dedicated hardware button and shown at the bottom of the screen. With Android 3, it moved to the top and became a vertical list. Some elements could be made available permanently as actions. In a way, the options menu and the action bar merged. While originally, all the aspects of the action bar were handled by the hosting activity, the `AppCompat` support library introduced an alternative implementation (`getSupportActionBar()`). It is still widely used today as part of Jetpack.

Using Scaffold() to structure your screen

Jetpack Compose includes several app bar implementations that closely follow Material Design or Material You specifications. They can be added to a Compose UI through Scaffold(), a composable function that acts as an app frame or skeleton. The following code snippet is the root of the ComposeUnitConverter UI. It sets up the theme and then delegates it to Scaffold():

```
@Composable
fun ComposeUnitConverter(factory: ViewModelFactory) {
    val navController = rememberNavController()
    val menuItems = listOf("Item #1", "Item #2")
    val scaffoldState = rememberScaffoldState()
    val snackbarCoroutineScope = rememberCoroutineScope()
    ComposeUnitConverterTheme {
        Scaffold(scaffoldState = scaffoldState,
            topBar = {
                ComposeUnitConverterTopBar(menuItems) { s ->
                    snackbarCoroutineScope.launch {
                        scaffoldState.snackbarHostState.showSnackbar(s)
                    }
                }
            },
            bottomBar = {
                ComposeUnitConverterBottomBar(navController)
            }
        ) {
            ComposeUnitConverterNavHost(
                navController = navController,
                factory = factory
            )
        }
    }
}
```

`Scaffold()` implements the basic Material Design visual layout structure. You can add several other Material composables, such as `TopAppBar()` or `BottomNavigation()`. Google calls this a **slot API** because a composable function is customized by inserting another composable into an area or space (slot) of the parent. Passing an already configured child provides more flexibility than exposing (lots of) configuration parameters. Depending on which children you slot in, `Scaffold()` may need to remember different states. You can pass a `ScaffoldState`, which can be created with `rememberScaffoldState()`.

My example uses `ScaffoldState` to show a snack bar, a brief temporary message that appears toward the bottom of the screen. As `showSnackbar()` is a suspending function, it must be called from a coroutine or another suspending function. Therefore, we must create and remember a `CoroutineScope` using `rememberCoroutineScope()` and invoke its `launch {}` function.

In the next section, I will show you how to create a top app bar with an options menu.

Creating a top app bar

App bars at the top of the screen are implemented using `TopAppBar()`. You can provide a navigation icon, a title, and a list of actions here:

```
@Composable
fun ComposeUnitConverterTopBar(menuItems: List<String>,
                               onClick: (String) -> Unit) {
    var menuOpened by remember { mutableStateOf(false) }
    TopAppBar(title = {
        Text(text = stringResource(id = R.string.app_name))
    },
        actions = {
        Box {
            IconButton(onClick = {
                menuOpened = true
            }) {
                Icon(Icons.Default.MoreVert, "")
            }
            DropdownMenu(expanded = menuOpened,
                onDismissRequest = {
                    menuOpened = false
                }) {
```

```
menuItems.forEachIndexed { index, s ->
    if (index > 0) Divider()
    DropdownMenuItem(onClick = {
        menuOpened = false
        onClick(s)
    }) {
        Text(s)
    }
}
                }
            }
        }
    )
}
```

TopAppBar() has no specific API for an options menu. Instead, the menu is treated as an ordinary action. Actions are typically IconButton() composables. They are displayed at the end of the app bar in a horizontal row. An IconButton() receives an onClick callback and an optional enabled parameter, which controls if the user can interact with the UI element.

In my example, the callback only sets a Boolean mutable state (menuOpened) to false. As you will see shortly, this closes the menu. content (usually an icon) is drawn inside the button. The Icon() composable receives an instance of ImageVector and a content description. You can get icon data from the resources, but you should use predefined graphics if possible – in my example, Icons.Default.MoreVert. Next, let's learn how to display a menu.

A Material Design drop-down menu (DropdownMenu()) allows you to display multiple choices compactly. It usually appears when you interact with another element, such as a button. My example places DropdownMenu() in a Box() with an IconButton(), which determines the location on-screen. The expanded parameter makes the menu visible (open) or invisible (closed). onDismissRequest is called when the user requests to dismiss the menu, such as by tapping outside the menu's bounds.

The content should consist of DropdownMenuItem() composables. onClick is called when the corresponding menu item is clicked. Your code must make sure that the menu is closed. If possible, you should pass the domain logic to be executed as a parameter to make your code reusable and stateless. In my example, a snack bar is shown.

This concludes our look at top app bars. In the next section, I will show you how to use `BottomNavigation()` to navigate to different screens using the Compose version of Jetpack Navigation.

> **Please Note**
>
> To use the Compose version of Jetpack Navigation in your app, you must add an implementation dependency of `androidx.navigation:navigation-compose` to your module-level `build.gradle` file.

Adding navigation

`Scaffold()` allows you to put content in a slot at the bottom of the screen using its `bottomBar` parameter. This can, for example, be a `BottomAppBar()`. Material Design bottom app bars provide access to a bottom navigation drawer and up to four actions, including a floating action button. `ComposeUnitConverter` adds `BottomNavigation()` instead. Material Design bottom navigation bars allow movement between primary destinations in an app.

Defining screens

Conceptually, primary destinations are *screens*, something that, before Jetpack Compose, may have been displayed in separate activities. Here's how screens are defined in `ComposeUnitConverter`:

```
sealed class ComposeUnitConverterScreen(
    val route: String,
    @StringRes val label: Int,
    @DrawableRes val icon: Int
) {
    companion object {
        val screens = listOf(
            Temperature,
            Distances
        )
        const val route_temperature = "temperature"
        const val route_distances = "distances"
    }
}
```

```
private object Temperature : ComposeUnitConverterScreen(
  route_temperature,
  R.string.temperature,
  R.drawable.baseline_thermostat_24
)

private object Distances : ComposeUnitConverterScreen(
  route_distances,
  R.string.distances,
  R.drawable.baseline_square_foot_24
)
}
```

ComposeUnitConverter consists of two screens – Temperature and Distances. route uniquely identifies a screen. label and icon are shown to the user. Let's see how this is done:

```
@Composable
fun ComposeUnitConverterBottomBar(navController:
  NavHostController) {
  BottomNavigation {
    val navBackStackEntry by
        navController.currentBackStackEntryAsState()
    val currentDestination = navBackStackEntry?.destination
    ComposeUnitConverterScreen.screens.forEach { screen ->
      BottomNavigationItem(
        selected = currentDestination?.hierarchy?.any {
          it.route == screen.route } == true,
        onClick = {
          navController.navigate(screen.route) {
            launchSingleTop = true
          }
        },
        label = {
          Text(text = stringResource(id = screen.label))
        },
```

```
icon = {
    Icon(
        painter = painterResource(id = screen.icon),
        contentDescription = stringResource(id =
            screen.label)
    )
},
alwaysShowLabel = false
    )
}
}
}
```

The content of `BottomNavigation()` consists of `BottomNavigationItem()` items. Each item represents a *destination*. We can add them with a simple loop:

```
ComposeUnitConverterScreen.screens.forEach { screen ->
```

As you can see, the `label` and `icon` properties of a `ComposeUnitConverterScreen` instance are used during the invocation of `BottomNavigationItem()`. `alwaysShowLabel` controls if the label is visible when an item is selected. An item will be selected if the corresponding screen is currently displayed. When a `BottomNavigationItem()` is clicked, its `onClick` callback is invoked. My implementation calls `navigate()` on the provided `NavHostController` instance, passing `route` from the corresponding `ComposeUnitConverterScreen` object.

So far, we have defined screens and mapped them to `BottomNavigationItem()` items. When an item is clicked, the app navigates to a given route. But how do routes relate to composable functions? I will show you in the next section.

Using NavHostController and NavHost()

An instance of `NavHostController` allows us to navigate to different screens by calling its `navigate()` function. We can obtain a reference to it inside `ComposeUnitConverter()` by invoking `rememberNavController()`, and then passing it to `ComposeUnitConverterBottomBar()`. The mapping between a route and a composable function is established through `NavHost()`. It belongs to the `androidx.navigation.compose` package. Here's how this composable is invoked:

```
@Composable
fun ComposeUnitConverterNavHost(
```

```
   navController: NavHostController,
   factory: ViewModelProvider.Factory?
) {
  NavHost(
    navController = navController,
    startDestination =
        ComposeUnitConverterScreen.route_temperature
  ) {
    composable(ComposeUnitConverterScreen.route_temperature) {
      TemperatureConverter(
        viewModel = viewModel(factory = factory)
      )
    }
    composable(ComposeUnitConverterScreen.route_distances) {
      DistancesConverter(
        viewModel = viewModel(factory = factory)
      )
    }
  }
}
```

NavHost() receives three parameters:

- A reference to our NavHostController
- The route for the start destination
- The builder that was used to construct the navigation graph

Before Jetpack Compose, the navigation graph was usually defined through an XML file. NavGraphBuilder provides access to a simple domain-specific language. composable() adds a composable function as a destination. Besides the route, you can pass a list of arguments and a list of deep links.

> **Tip**
> A detailed description of Jetpack Navigation is beyond the scope of this book.
> You can find more information at https://developer.android.
> com/guide/navigation.

Summary

This chapter showcased how key elements of Jetpack Compose work together in a real-world app. You learned how to theme Compose apps and how to keep your Compose theme in sync with resource-based themes.

I also showed you how `Scaffold()` acts as an app frame or skeleton. We used its slot API to plug in a top app bar with a menu, as well as a bottom bar to navigate between screens using the Compose version of Jetpack Navigation.

In the next chapter, *Tips, Tricks, and Best Practices*, we will discuss how to separate UI and business logic. We will revisit `ComposeUnitConverter`, this time focusing on its use of ViewModels.

7
Tips, Tricks, and Best Practices

In *Chapter 6*, *Putting Pieces Together*, we combined several key techniques of Jetpack Compose such as state hoisting, app theming, and navigation in a real-world example. `ComposeUnitConverter` stores state in a `ViewModel` and eventually persists it using the *Repository* pattern. In this chapter, I show you how to pass objects to a `ViewModel` upon instantiation and use these objects to load and save data. In *Chapter 3*, *Exploring the Key Principles of Compose*, we examined features of well-behaved composable functions. Composables should be free of side effects to make them reusable and easy to test. However, there are situations when you need to either react to or initiate state changes that happen outside the scope of a composable function. We will cover this at the end of this chapter.

These are the main sections of this chapter:

- Persisting and retrieving state
- Keeping your composables responsive
- Understanding side effects

We start by continuing the exploration of the `ViewModel` pattern we began in the *Using a ViewModel* section of *Chapter 5, Managing the State of Your Composable Functions*. This time, we will add business logic to the `ViewModel` and inject an object that can persist and retrieve data.

The *Keeping your composables responsive* section revisits one of the key requirements of a composable function. As recomposition can occur very often, composables must be as fast as possible. This greatly influences what the code may and may not do. Long-running tasks—for example, complex computations or network calls—should not be invoked synchronously.

The *Understanding side effects* section covers situations when you need to either react to or initiate state changes that happen outside the scope of a composable function. For example, we will be using `LaunchedEffect` to start and stop complex computations.

Technical requirements

The *Persisting and retrieving state* and *Keeping your composables responsive* sections further discuss the sample `ComposeUnitConverter` app. The *Understanding side effects* section is based on the `EffectDemo` sample. Please refer to the *Technical requirements* section of *Chapter 1, Building Your First Compose App* for information about how to install and set up Android Studio and how to get the repository accompanying this book.

All the code files for this chapter can be found on GitHub at `https://github.com/PacktPublishing/Android-UI-Development-with-Jetpack-Compose/tree/main/chapter_07`.

Persisting and retrieving state

State is app data that may change over time. In a Compose app, state is typically represented as instances of `State` or `MutableState`. If such objects are used inside composable functions, a recomposition is triggered upon state changes. If a state is passed to several composables, all of them may be recomposed. This leads to the *state hoisting* principle: state is passed to composable functions rather than being remembered inside them. Often, such state is remembered in the composable that is the parent of the ones using the state. An alternative approach is to implement an architectural pattern called `ViewModel`. It is used in many **user interface** (**UI**) frameworks on various platforms. On Android, it has been available since 2017 as part of the **Android Architecture Components**.

The general idea of a `ViewModel` is to combine data and access logic that is specific to a certain part of an app. Depending on the platform, this may be a screen, a window, a dialog, or another similar top-level container. On Android, it's usually an activity. The data is observable, so UI elements can register and get notified upon changes. How the observable pattern is implemented depends on the platform. The Android Architecture Components introduced `LiveData` and `MutableLiveData`. In the *Surviving configuration changes* section of *Chapter 5*, *Managing the State of Your Composable Functions*, I showed you how to use them inside a `ViewModel` to store data that survives device rotations and how to connect `LiveData` instances to composable functions.

Here's a brief recap: to connect `LiveData` objects to the Compose world, we first obtain a `ViewModel` instance using `androidx.lifecycle.viewmodel.compose.viewModel()`, and then invoke the `observeAsState()` extension function on a property of the `ViewModel`. The returned state is read-only, so if a composable wants to update the property, it must call a setter that needs to be provided by the `ViewModel`.

So far, I have not explained how to persist state and restore it later. To put it another way: where do `ViewModel` instances get the initial values for their data, and what do they do upon changes? Let's find out in the next section.

Injecting objects into a ViewModel

If a `ViewModel` wants to load and save data, it may need to access a database, the local filesystem, or some remote web service. Yet, it should be irrelevant for the `ViewModel` how reading and writing data works behind the scenes. The Android Architecture Components suggest implementing the *Repository* pattern. A repository abstracts the mechanics of loading and saving data and makes it available through a collection-like interface. You can find out more about the Repository pattern at `https://martinfowler.com/eaaCatalog/repository.html`.

You will see shortly what the implementation of a simple repository may look like, but first, I need to show you how to pass objects to a `ViewModel` upon instantiation. `viewModel()` receives a `factory` parameter of type `ViewModelProvider.Factory`. It is used to create `ViewModel` instances. If you pass `null` (the default value), a built-in default factory is used. `ComposeUnitConverter` has two screens, so its factory must be able to create `ViewModel` instances for each screen.

Here's what `ViewModelFactory` looks like:

```
class ViewModelFactory(private val repository: Repository)
  :ViewModelProvider.NewInstanceFactory() {
  override fun <T : ViewModel?> create(modelClass:
```

```
Class<T>): T =
    if (modelClass.isAssignableFrom
    (TemperatureViewModel::class.java))
        TemperatureViewModel(repository) as T
    else
        DistancesViewModel(repository) as T
}
```

ViewModelFactory extends the ViewModelProvider.NewInstanceFactory static class and overrides the create() method (which belongs to the parent Factory interface). The modelClass represents the ViewModel to be created. Therefore, if the following code is true, then we instantiate TemperatureViewModel and pass repository:

```
modelClass.isAssignableFrom
    (TemperatureViewModel::class.java)
```

This parameter was passed to the constructor of ViewModelFactory. Otherwise, a DistancesViewModel instance is created. Its constructor also receives repository. If your factory needs to differentiate between more ViewModel instances, you will probably use a when instead.

Next, let's look at my Repository class to find out how ComposeUnitConverter loads and saves data. You can see this in the following code snippet:

```
class Repository(context: Context) {
    private val prefs =
        PreferenceManager.getDefaultSharedPreferences(context)
    fun getInt(key: String, default: Int) =
        prefs.getInt(key, default)
    fun putInt(key: String, value: Int) {
        prefs.edit().putInt(key, value).apply()
    }
    fun getString(key: String,
        default: String) = prefs.getString(key, default)
```

```
fun putString(key: String, value: String) {
    prefs.edit().putString(key, value).apply()
}
}
```

`Repository` uses Jetpack Preference. This library is a replacement for the platform classes and interfaces inside the `android.preference` package, which was deprecated with **application programming interface (API)** level 29.

> **Important Note**
> Both the platform classes and the library are designed for user settings. You should not use them to access more complex data, larger texts, or images. Record-like data is best kept in an SQLite database, whereas files are ideal for large texts or images.

To use Jetpack Preference, we need to add an implementation dependency to `androidx. preference:preference-ktx` in the module-level `build.gradle` file. `getDefaultSharedPreferences()` requires an instance of `android.content. Context`, which is passed to the constructor of `Repository`.

Before we move on, let's recap what I showed you so far, as follows:

- `TemperatureViewModel` and `DistancesViewModel` receive a `Repository` instance in their constructor.
- `Repository` receives a `Context` object.
- `ViewModel` instances are decoupled from activities. They survive configuration changes.

The last bullet point has an important consequence regarding the context we can pass to the repository. Let's find out more in the next section.

Using the factory

Here's how both the repository and factory are created:

```
class ComposeUnitConverterActivity : ComponentActivity() {
    override fun onCreate(savedInstanceState: Bundle?) {
        super.onCreate(savedInstanceState)
```

```
val factory =
    ViewModelFactory(Repository(applicationContext))
setContent {
    ComposeUnitConverter(factory)
  }
 }
}
```

Both `Repository` and `ViewModelFactory` are ordinary objects, so they are simply instantiated, passing the required parameters to them.

> **Important Note**
>
> It may be tempting to pass `this` (the calling activity) as the context.
> However, as `ViewModel` instances survive configuration changes (that
> is, the recreation of an activity), the context may change. If it does, the
> repository would be accessing a no longer available activity. By using
> `applicationContext`, we make sure that this issue does not occur.

`ComposeUnitConverter()` is the root of the composable hierarchy. It passes the factory to `ComposeUnitConverterNavHost()`, which in turn uses it inside `composable {}` as a parameter for the screens, as illustrated in the following code snippet:

```
composable(ComposeUnitConverterScreen.route_temperature) {
    TemperatureConverter(
        viewModel = viewModel(factory = factory)
    )
}
```

In this section, I showed you how to inject a repository object into a `ViewModel` using simple constructor invocation. If your app relies on a **dependency injection (DI)** framework, you will need to use its mechanisms (for example, an annotation) instead. However, this is beyond the scope of this book. Next, we will look at how the `ViewModel` uses the repository.

Keeping your composables responsive

When implementing composable functions, you should always keep in mind that their main purpose is to declare the UI and to handle user interactions. Ideally, anything needed to achieve this is passed to the composable, including state and logic (such as click handlers), making it stateless. If state is needed only inside a composable, the function may keep state temporarily using `remember` { }. Such composables are called **stateful**. If data is kept in a `ViewModel`, composables must interact with it. So, the `ViewModel` code must be fast, too.

Communicating with ViewModel instances

Data inside a `ViewModel` should be observable. `ComposeUnitConverter` uses `LiveData` and `MutableLiveData` from the Android Architecture Components to achieve this. You can choose other implementations of the *Observer* pattern, provided there is a way to obtain `State` or `MutableState` instances that are updated upon changes in the `ViewModel`. This is beyond the scope of this book. `TemperatureViewModel` is the `ViewModel` for the `TemperatureConverter()` composable function.

Let's look at its implementation. In the following code snippet, I omitted code related to the `scale` property for brevity. You can find the full implementation in the GitHub repository:

```
class TemperatureViewModel(private val repository:
  Repository) : ViewModel() {
  ...

  private val _temperature: MutableLiveData<String>
          = MutableLiveData(
              repository.getString("temperature", "")
  )

  val temperature: LiveData<String>
    get() = _temperature

  fun getTemperatureAsFloat(): Float
          = (_temperature.value ?: "").let {
    return try {
      it.toFloat()
    } catch (e: NumberFormatException) {
      Float.NaN
```

```
    }
  }

  fun setTemperature(value: String) {
    _temperature.value = value
    repository.putString("temperature", value)
  }

  fun convert() = getTemperatureAsFloat().let {
    if (!it.isNaN())
      if (_scale.value == R.string.celsius)
        (it * 1.8F) + 32F
      else
        (it - 32F) / 1.8F
    else
      Float.NaN
  }
}
```

`ViewModel` instances present their data through pairs of variables, as follows:

- A public read-only property (`temperature`)
- A private writeable backing variable (`_temperature`)

Properties are not changed by assigning a new value but by invoking some setter functions (`setTemperature()`). You can find an explanation of why this is the case in the *Using a ViewModel* section of *Chapter 5, Managing the State of Your Composable Functions*. There may be additional functions that can be invoked by the composable—for example, logic to convert a temperature from °C to °F (`convert()`) should not be part of the composable code. The same applies to format conversions (from `String` to `Float`). These are best kept in the `ViewModel`.

Here's how the `ViewModel` is used from a composable function:

```
@Composable
fun TemperatureConverter(viewModel: TemperatureViewModel) {
  ...
  val currentValue = viewModel.temperature.observeAsState(
                     viewModel.temperature.value ?: "")
```

```kotlin
val scale = viewModel.scale.observeAsState(
                viewModel.scale.value ?: R.string.celsius)
var result by remember { mutableStateOf("") }
val calc = {
  val temp = viewModel.convert()
  result = if (temp.isNaN())
    ""
  else
    "$temp${
      if (scale.value == R.string.celsius)
        strFahrenheit
      else strCelsius
    }"
}
...
Column(
  ...
) {
  TemperatureTextField(
    temperature = currentValue,
    modifier = Modifier.padding(bottom = 16.dp),
    callback = calc,
    viewModel = viewModel
  )
  ...
  Button(
    onClick = calc,
    ...
  if (result.isNotEmpty()) {
    Text(
      text = result,
      style = MaterialTheme.typography.h3
    )
  }
  ...
```

Have you noticed that TemperatureConverter() receives its ViewModel as
a parameter?

> **Tip**
>
> You should provide a default value (viewModel()) for preview and
> testability, if possible. However, this doesn't work if the ViewModel requires
> a repository (as in my example) or other constructor values.

State instances are obtained by invoking observeAsState() of ViewModel
properties (temperature and scale), which are LiveData instances. The code
assigned to calc is executed when either the **Convert** button or **Done** button of the
virtual keyboard is pressed. It creates a string representing the converted temperature,
including scale, and assigns it to result, a state being used in a Text() composable.
Please note that the calc lambda expression calls the convert() function of
ViewModel function to get the converted temperature. You should always try to remove
business logic from composables and instead put it inside the ViewModel.

So far, I showed you how to observe changes in the ViewModel and how to invoke
logic inside it. There is one piece left: changing a property. In the preceding code snippet,
TemperatureTextField() receives the ViewModel. Let's see what it does with
it here:

```
@Composable
fun TemperatureTextField(
    temperature: State<String>,
    modifier: Modifier = Modifier,
    callback: () -> Unit,
    viewModel: TemperatureViewModel
) {
    TextField(
        value = temperature.value,
        onValueChange = {
            viewModel.setTemperature(it)
        },
        ...
```

Whenever the text changes, setTemperature() is invoked with the new value. Please
recall that the setter does the following:

```
_temperature.value = value
```

The `ViewModel` updates the value of the `_temperature` (`MutableLiveData`) backing variable. As the `temperature` public property references `_temperature`, its observers (in my example, the state returned by `observeAsState()` in `TemperatureConverter()`) are notified. This triggers a recomposition.

In this section, we focused on how communication flows between composable functions and `ViewModel` instances. Next, we examine what can go wrong if the `ViewModel` breaks the contract with the composable and what you can do to prevent this.

Handling long-running tasks

Composable functions actively interact with a `ViewModel` by setting new values for properties (`setTemperature()`) and by invoking functions that implement business logic (`convert()`). As recompositions can occur frequently, these functions may be called very often. Consequently, they must return very fast. This surely is the case for simple arithmetic, such as converting between °C and °F.

On the other hand, some algorithms may become increasingly time-consuming for certain inputs. Here's an example. Fibonacci numbers can be computed recursively and iteratively. While a recursive algorithm is simpler to implement, it takes much longer for large numbers. If a synchronous function call does not return in a timely fashion, it may affect how the user perceives your app. You can test this by adding `while (true) ;` as the first line of code inside `convert()`. If you then run `ComposeUnitConverter`, enter some number, and press **Convert**, the app will no longer respond.

> **Important Note**
> Potentially long-running tasks must be implemented asynchronously.

To avoid situations where the app is not responding because a computation takes too much time, you must decouple the computation from delivering the result. This is done with just a few steps, as follows:

1. Provide the result as an observable property.
2. Compute the result using a coroutine or a Kotlin flow.
3. Once the computation is finished, update the `result` property.

Here's a sample implementation taken from `DistancesViewModel`:

```
private val _convertedDistance: MutableLiveData<Float>
                = MutableLiveData(Float.NaN)
```

```
val convertedDistance: LiveData<Float>
  get() = _convertedDistance


fun convert() {
  getDistanceAsFloat().let {
    viewModelScope.launch {
      _convertedDistance.value = if (!it.isNaN())
        if (_unit.value == R.string.meter)
          it * 0.00062137F
        else
          it / 0.00062137F
      else
        Float.NaN
    }
  }
}
```

viewModelScope is available via an implementation dependency to `androidx.lifecycle:lifecycle-viewmodel-ktx` in the module-level `build.gradle` file. `convert()` spawns a coroutine, which will update the value of `_convertedDistance` once the computation is finished. Composable functions can observe changes by invoking `observeAsState()` on the `convertedDistance` public property. But how do you access `convertedDistance` and `convert()`? Here's a code snippet from `DistancesConverter.kt`:

```
val convertedValue by
        viewModel.convertedDistance.observeAsState()
val result by remember(convertedValue) {
  mutableStateOf(
    if (convertedValue?.isNaN() != false)
      ""
    else
      "$convertedValue ${
        if (unit.value == R.string.meter)
          strMile
        else strMeter
      }"
  )
```

```
}
val calc = {
    viewModel.convert()
}
```

`result` receives the text to be output once a distance has been converted, so it should update itself whenever `convertedValue` changes. Therefore, I pass `convertedValue` as a key to `remember {}`. Whenever the key changes, the `mutableStateOf()` lambda expression is recomputed, so `result` gets updated. `calc` is invoked when the **Convert** button or the **Done** button on the virtual keyboard is pressed. It spawns an asynchronous operation, which eventually will update `convertedValue`.

In this section, I have often used the term *computation*. Computation does not only mean arithmetic. Accessing databases, files, or web services may also consume considerable resources and be time-consuming. Such operations must be executed asynchronously. Please keep in mind that long-running tasks may not be part of the `ViewModel` itself but be invoked from it (for example, a repository). Consequently, such code must be fast too. My `Repository` implementation accesses the `Preferences` API synchronously for simplicity. Strictly speaking, even such basic operations should be asynchronous.

> **Tip**
>
> Jetpack DataStore allows you to store key-value pairs or typed objects with protocol buffers. It uses Kotlin coroutines and Flow to store data asynchronously. You can find more information about Jetpack DataStore at `https://developer.android.com/topic/libraries/architecture/datastore`.

This concludes our look at the communication between composable functions and `ViewModel` instances. In the next section, I will introduce you to composables that do not emit UI elements but cause side effects to run when a composition completes.

Understanding side effects

In the *Using Scaffold() to structure your screen* section of *Chapter 6, Putting Pieces Together*, I showed you how to display a snack bar using `rememberCoroutineScope {}` and `scaffoldState.snackbarHostState.showSnackbar()`. As `showSnackbar()` is a suspending function, it must be called from a coroutine or another suspending function. Therefore, we created and remembered `CoroutineScope` using `rememberCoroutineScope()` and invoked its `launch {}` function.

Invoking suspending functions

The `LaunchedEffect()` composable is an alternative approach for spawning a suspending function. To see how it works, let's look at the `LaunchedEffectDemo()` composable. It belongs to the `EffectDemo` sample, as illustrated in the following screenshot:

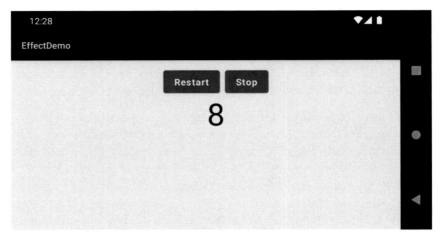

Figure 7.1 – The EffectDemo sample showing LaunchedEffectDemo()

`LaunchedEffectDemo()` implements a counter. Once the **Start** button has been clicked, a counter is incremented every second. Clicking on **Restart** resets the counter. **Stop** terminates it. The code to achieve this is illustrated in the following snippet:

```
@Composable
fun LaunchedEffectDemo() {
    var clickCount by rememberSaveable { mutableStateOf(0) }
    var counter by rememberSaveable { mutableStateOf(0) }
    Column(
        modifier = Modifier
            .fillMaxSize()
            .padding(16.dp),
        horizontalAlignment = Alignment.CenterHorizontally
    ) {
        Row {
            Button(onClick = {
                clickCount += 1
            }) {
                Text(
```

```
                          text = if (clickCount == 0)
                              stringResource(id = R.string.start)
                          else
                              stringResource(id = R.string.restart)
                      )
                  }
                  Spacer(modifier = Modifier.width(8.dp))
                  Button(enabled = clickCount > 0,
                      onClick = {
                          clickCount = 0
                      }) {
                      Text(text = stringResource(id =
                                      R.string.stop))
                  }
                  if (clickCount > 0) {
                      LaunchedEffect(clickCount) {
                          counter = 0
                          while (isActive) {
                              counter += 1
                              delay(1000)
                          }
                      }
                  }
              }
              Text(
                  text = "$counter",
                  style = MaterialTheme.typography.h3
              )
          }
      }
```

clickCount counts how often **Start** or **Restart** has been clicked. **Stop** resets it to 0. A value greater than 0 indicates that another remembered variable (counter) should be increased every second. This is done by a suspending function that is passed to LaunchedEffect(). This composable is used to safely call suspend functions from inside a composable. Let's see how it works.

When `LaunchedEffect()` enters the composition (`if (clickCount > 0) ...`), it launches a coroutine with the block of code passed as a parameter. The coroutine will be cancelled if `LaunchedEffect()` leaves the composition (`clickCount <= 0`). Have you noticed that it receives one parameter? If `LaunchedEffect()` is recomposed with different keys (my example uses just one, but you can pass more if needed), the existing coroutine will be canceled and a new one is started.

As you have seen, `LaunchedEffect()` makes it easy to start and restart asynchronous tasks. The corresponding coroutines are cleaned up automatically. But what if you need to do some additional housekeeping (such as unregistering listeners) when keys change or when the composable leaves the composition? Let's find out in the next section.

Cleaning up with DisposableEffect()

The `DisposableEffect()` composable function runs code when its key changes. Additionally, you can pass a lambda expression for cleanup purposes. It will be executed when the `DisposableEffect()` function leaves the composition. The code is illustrated in the following snippet:

```
DisposableEffect(clickCount) {
    println("init: clickCount is $clickCount")
    onDispose {
        println("dispose: clickCount is $clickCount")
    }
}
```

A message starting with `init:` will be printed each time `clickCount` changes (that is, when **Start** or **Restart** is clicked). A message starting with `dispose:` will appear when `clickCount` changes or when `DisposableEffect()` leaves the composition.

> **Important Note**
> `DisposableEffect()` *must* include an `onDispose {}` clause as the final statement in its block.

I have given you two hands-on examples that use side effects in a Compose app. The `Effect` APIs contain several other useful composables—for example, you can use `SideEffect()` to publish Compose state to non-Compose parts of your app, and `produceState()` allows you to convert non-Compose state into `State` instances.

You can find additional information about the `Effect` APIs at `https://developer.android.com/jetpack/compose/side-effects`.

Summary

This chapter covered additional aspects of the `ComposeUnitConverter` example. We continued the exploration of the `ViewModel` pattern we began looking at in the *Using a ViewModel* section of *Chapter 5, Managing the State of Your Composable Functions*. This time, we added business logic to the `ViewModel` and injected an object that can persist and retrieve data.

The *Keeping your composables responsive* section revisited one of the key requirements of a composable function. Recomposition can occur very often, therefore composables must be as fast as possible, which dictates what code inside them may and may not do. I showed you how a simple loop can cause a Compose app to stop responding, and how coroutines counteract this.

In the final main section, *Understanding side effects*, we examined so-called side effects and used `LaunchedEffect` to implement a simple counter.

In *Chapter 8, Working with Animations*, you will learn how to show and hide UI elements with animations. We will spice up transitions through visual effects and use animation to visualize state changes.

Part 3: Advanced Topics

This part focuses on how to improve the quality of Compose apps, for example, by enhancing their visual appeal through animations. It also illustrates how and why to test composable functions, and how to mix composables with old-fashioned Views.

We will cover the following chapters in this section:

8
Working with Animations

In the previous chapters, I introduced you to many technical aspects of Jetpack Compose and showed you how to write well-behaving and good-looking apps. Now, adding animations and transitions will make your apps really shine! Compose simplifies the process of adding animation effects greatly over the old View-based approach.

In this chapter, you will learn important animation-related application programming interfaces, see animations of single and multiple properties, as well as transitions between composables in action, and master the relationship between state changes and visual interactions.

The main sections of this chapter are as follows:

- Using animation to visualize state changes
- Showing and hiding UI elements with animations
- Spicing up transitions through visual effects

We start by using animations to visualize state changes. Think of a simple use case: clicking a button might change the color of a UI object. But, just switching between colors feels somewhat abrupt, whereas a gradual change is much more visually pleasing. Also, if you want to change several values during the animation, Jetpack Compose can do that easily, too. I'll introduce you to the `updateTransition()` composable, which is used in such scenarios.

The *Showing and hiding UI elements with animations* section introduces you to the `AnimatedVisibility()` composable function. It allows you to apply enter and exit transitions, which will be played back while the content appears or disappears. We will also animate size changes and learn about the corresponding `animateContentSize()` modifier.

In the *Spicing up transitions through visual effects* section, we will be using the `Crossfade()` composable to switch between two layouts with a crossfade animation. Furthermore, you will learn about `AnimationSpec`. This interface represents the specification of an animation. A take on infinite animations concludes the section.

Technical requirements

This chapter is based on the `AnimationDemo` sample. Please refer to the *Technical requirements* section in *Chapter 1, Building Your First Compose App,* for information about how to install and set up Android Studio, and how to get the repository accompanying this book.

All the code files for this chapter can be found on GitHub at `https://github.com/PacktPublishing/Android-UI-Development-with-Jetpack-Compose/tree/main/chapter_08`.

Using animation to visualize state changes

State is app data that may change over time. In a Compose app, state (for example, a color) is represented through `State` or `MutableState` instances. State changes trigger recompositions. The following example shows a button and a box. Clicking the button toggles the color of the box between red and white by changing state:

```
@Composable
fun StateChangeDemo() {
  var toggled by remember {
    mutableStateOf(false)
  }
  val color = if (toggled)
    Color.White
  else
    Color.Red
  Column(
    modifier = Modifier
```

```
        .fillMaxSize()
        .padding(16.dp),
    horizontalAlignment = Alignment.CenterHorizontally
) {
    Button(onClick = {
        toggled = !toggled
    }) {
        Text(
            stringResource(R.string.toggle)
        )
    }
    Box(
        modifier = Modifier
            .padding(top = 32.dp)
            .background(color = color)
            .size(128.dp)
    )
    }
}
```

In this example, `color` is a simple immutable variable. It is set each time `toggled` (a mutable `Boolean` state) changes (this happens inside `onClick`). As `color` is used with a modifier applied to `Box()` (`background(color = color)`), clicking the button changes the box color.

If you try the code, the switch feels very sudden and abrupt. This is because white and red are not very similar. Using an animation will make the change much more pleasant. Let's see how this works.

Animating single value changes

To animate a color, you can use the built-in `animateColorAsState()` composable. Replace the `val color = if (toggled) …` assignment inside `StateDemo()` with the following code block. If you want to try it out, you can find a composable function called `SingleValueAnimationDemo()` in `AnimationDemoActivity.kt`, which belongs to the `AnimationDemo` sample:

```
val color by animateColorAsState(
    targetValue = if (toggled)
        Color.White
```

```
    else
        Color.Red
)
```

`animateColorAsState()` returns a `State<Color>` instance. Whenever `targetValue` changes, the animation will run automatically. If the change occurs while the animation is in progress, the ongoing animation will adjust to match the new target value.

> **Tip**
> Using the by keyword, you can access the color state like ordinary variables.

You can provide an optional listener to get notified when the animation is finished. The following line of code prints the color that matches the new state:

```
finishedListener = { color -> println(color) }
```

To customize your animation, you can pass an instance of `AnimationSpec<Color>` to `animateColorAsState()`. The default value is `colorDefaultSpring`, a private value in `SingleValueAnimation.kt`:

```
private val colorDefaultSpring = spring<Color>()
```

`spring()` is a top-level function in `AnimationSpec.kt`. It receives a damping ratio, a stiffness, and a visibility threshold. The following line of code makes the color animation very soft:

```
animationSpec = spring(stiffness = Spring.StiffnessVeryLow)
```

`spring()` returns `SpringSpec`. This class implements the `FiniteAnimationSpec` interface, which in turn extends `AnimationSpec`. This interface defines the specification of an animation, which includes the data type to be animated and the animation configuration, in this case, a spring metaphor. There are others. We will be returning to this interface in the *Spicing up transitions through visual effects* section. Next, we look at animating multiple value changes.

Animating multiple value changes

In this section, I will show you how to animate several values at once upon a state change. The setup is similar to `StateDemo()` and `SingleValueAnimationDemo()`: a `Column()` instance contains a `Button()` instance and a `Box()` instance. But this time, the content of the box is `Text()`. The button toggles a state, which starts the animation.

The following version of `MultipleValuesAnimationDemo()` does not yet contain an animation. It will be inserted below the comment reading **FIXME: animation setup missing**:

```
@Composable
fun MultipleValuesAnimationDemo() {
  var toggled by remember {
    mutableStateOf(false)
  }
  // FIXME: animation setup missing
  Column(
    modifier = Modifier
      .fillMaxSize()
      .padding(16.dp),
    horizontalAlignment = Alignment.CenterHorizontally
  ) {
    Button(onClick = {
      toggled = !toggled
    }) {
      Text(
        stringResource(R.string.toggle)
      )
    }
    Box(
      contentAlignment = Alignment.Center,
      modifier = Modifier
        .padding(top = 32.dp)
        .border(
          width = borderWidth,
          color = Color.Black
        )
        .size(128.dp)
    ) {
      Text(
        text = stringResource(id = R.string.app_name),
        modifier = Modifier.rotate(degrees = degrees)
      )
```

```
        }
    }
}
```

The `Box()` shows a black border, whose width is controlled by `borderWidth`. To apply borders to your composable functions, just add the `border()` modifier. `Text()` is rotated. You can achieve this with the `rotate()` modifier. The `degrees` variable holds the angle. `degrees` and `borderWidth` will change during the animation. Here's how this is done:

```
val transition = updateTransition(targetState = toggled)
val borderWidth by transition.animateDp() { state ->
    if (state)
        10.dp
    else
        1.dp
}
val degrees by transition.animateFloat() { state ->
    if (state) -90F
    else
        0F
}
```

The `updateTransition()` composable function configures and returns a `Transition`. When `targetState` changes, the transition will run all of its child animations toward their target values. Child animations are added using `animate...()` functions. They are not part of a `Transition` instance but are extension functions. `animateDp()` adds an animation based on density-independent pixels.

In my example, it controls the border width. `animateFloat()` creates a `Float` animation. This function is ideal for changing the rotation of `Text()`, which is a `Float` value. There are more `animate...()` functions, which operate on other data types. For example, `animateInt()` works with `Int` values. `animateOffset()` animates an `Offset` instance. You can find them in the `Transition.kt` file, which belongs to the `androidx.compose.animation.core` package.

`Transition` instances provide several properties reflecting the status of a transition. For example, `isRunning` indicates whether any animation in the transition is currently running. `segment` contains the initial state and the target state of the currently ongoing transition. The current state of the transition is available through `currentState`. This will be the initial state until the transition is finished. Then, `currentState` is set to the target state.

As you have seen, it is very easy to use state changes to trigger animations. So far, these animations have modified the visual appearance of one or more composable functions. In the next section, I will show you how to apply animations while showing or hiding UI elements.

Showing and hiding UI elements with animations

Often, your UI will contain information that need not be visible all the time. For example, in an address book you may want to show only key attributes of a contact, and present detailed information upon request, typically after a button click. However, just showing and hiding the additional data feels sudden and abrupt. Using animations leads to a more pleasant experience, so let's look into this more.

Understanding AnimatedVisibility()

In this section, we will look at my sample composable `AnimatedVisibilityDemo()`. It belongs to the `AnimationDemo` project. Like `StateDemo()`, `SingleValueAnimationDemo()`, and `MultipleValuesAnimationDemo()`, it uses a `Column()` instance, which contains a `Button()` instance and a `Box()` instance. This part of the code is simple and straightforward, so there is no need to repeat it in print. The button toggles a state, which starts the animation. Let's see how this works:

```
AnimatedVisibility(
    visible = visible,
    enter = slideInHorizontally(),
    exit = slideOutVertically()
) {
    Box(
        modifier = Modifier
            .padding(top = 32.dp)
            .background(color = Color.Red)
            .size(128.dp)
    )
}
```

The box is wrapped in `AnimatedVisibility()`. This built-in composable function animates the appearance and disappearance of its content, when the `visible` parameter changes. You can specify different `EnterTransition` and `ExitTransition` instances. In my example, the box enters by sliding in horizontally and exits by sliding out vertically.

Currently, there are three transition types:

- Fade

- Expand and shrink

- Slide

They can be combined using +:

```
enter = slideInHorizontally() + fadeIn(),
```

The combination order doesn't matter as the animations start simultaneously.

If you do not pass a value for `enter`, the content will default to fading in while expanding vertically. Omitting `exit` will cause the content to fade out while shrinking vertically.

> **Please Note**
>
> At the time of writing, `AnimatedVisibility()` is experimental. To use it in your app, you must add the `@ExperimentalAnimationApi` annotation. This will change with Jetpack Compose 1.1.

In this section, I showed you how to animate the appearance and disappearance of content. A variation of this subject is to visualize size changes (if either `width`, `height`, or both are 0, the UI element is no longer visible). Let's find out how to do this in the following section.

Animating size changes

Sometimes you may want to change the amount of space a UI element requires onscreen. Think of text fields. In compact mode, your app could show only three lines, whereas in detail mode it might display 10 lines or more. My `SizeChangeAnimationDemo()` sample composable (*Figure 8.1*) uses a slider to control the `maxLines` value of `Text()`:

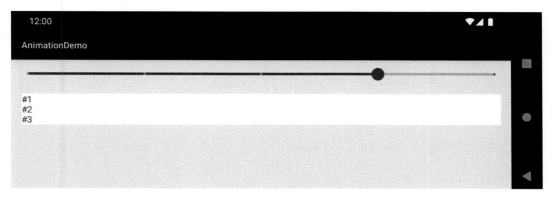

Figure 8.1 – The AnimationDemo sample showing SizeChangeAnimationDemo()

The general setup follows the examples from the previous sections: a Column() instance acts as a container for some composable functions, in this case a Slider() instance and a Text() instance. Then a state change triggers the animation. Here is the code:

```
@Composable
fun SizeChangeAnimationDemo() {
  var size by remember { mutableStateOf(1F) }
  Column(
    modifier = Modifier
      .fillMaxSize()
      .padding(16.dp)
  ) {
    Slider(
      value = size,
      valueRange = (1F..4F),
      steps = 3,
      onValueChange = {
        size = it
      },
      modifier = Modifier.padding(bottom = 8.dp)
    )
    Text(
      text = stringResource(id = R.string.lines),
      modifier = Modifier
        .fillMaxWidth()
        .background(Color.White)
```

```
        .animateContentSize(),
    maxLines = size.toInt(),
    color = Color.Blue
  )
 }
}
```

`size` is a mutable `Float` state. It is passed to `Slider()` as its default value. When the slider is moved, `onValueChange { }` is invoked. The lambda expression receives the new value, which is assigned to `size`. The `Text()` composable uses the state as a value for `maxLines`.

The animation is handled by the `animateContentSize()` modifier. It belongs to the `androidx.compose.animation` package. The modifier expects two parameters, `animationSpec` and `finishedListener`. I introduced both briefly in the *Animating single value changes* section. `animationSpec` defaults to `spring()`. If you want the lines to appear all at once after some delay, you can add the following:

```
animationSpec = snap(1000)
```

A snap animation immediately switches the animating value to the end value. You pass the number of milliseconds to wait before the animation runs. It defaults to `0`. Now, `snap()` returns an instance of `SnapSpec`, an implementation of `AnimationSpec`. We will turn to this interface in the *Spicing up transitions through visual effects* section.

The default value of `finishedListener` is `null`. You can provide an implementation, if your app wants to get notified when the size change animation is finished. Both the initial value and the final size are passed to the listener. If the animation is interrupted, the initial value will be the size at the point of interruption. This helps determine the direction of the size change.

This concludes our look at showing and hiding UI elements with animations. In the next section, we focus on exchanging parts of the UI. For example, we will be using `Crossfade()` to switch between two composable functions with a crossfade animation.

Spicing up transitions through visual effects

So far, I have shown you animations that modify certain aspects of a UI element, like its color, size, or visibility. But sometimes you may want to *exchange* parts of your UI. Then, `Crossfade()` comes in handy. It allows you to switch between two composable functions with a crossfade animation. Let's look at my `CrossfadeAnimationDemo()` sample (*Figure 8.2*), part of the `AnimationDemo` project, to see how this works:

Figure 8.2 – The AnimationDemo sample showing CrossfadeAnimationDemo()

A switch toggles between two screens. As we are focusing on animation, I kept the
Screen() composable very simple, just a box with customizable background color, and a
big text centered inside. You can find its source code in AnimationDemoActivity.kt.

Crossfading composable functions

Like most examples in this chapter, CrossfadeAnimationDemo() uses a Column()
as the root element. The column contains a switch, and the screen to display. Which one is
shown depends on a mutable Boolean state:

```
@Composable
fun CrossfadeAnimationDemo() {
  var isFirstScreen by remember { mutableStateOf(true) }
  Column(
    modifier = Modifier
      .fillMaxSize(),
    horizontalAlignment = Alignment.CenterHorizontally
  ) {
    Switch(
      checked = isFirstScreen,
      onCheckedChange = {
```

```
            isFirstScreen = !isFirstScreen
        },
        modifier = Modifier.padding(top = 16.dp,
                                    bottom = 16.dp)
    )
    Crossfade(targetState = isFirstScreen) { it ->
        if (it) {
            Screen(
                text = stringResource(id = R.string.letter_w),
                backgroundColor = Color.Gray
            )
        } else {
            Screen(
                text = stringResource(id = R.string.letter_i),
                backgroundColor = Color.LightGray
            )
        }
    }
}
}
```

The onCheckedChange lambda expression of Switch() toggles isFirstScreen. This state is passed to Crossfade() as the targetState parameter. Like in the other animations I showed you so far, it triggers the animation every time the value changes. Specifically, the content called with the old value will be faded out, and the content called with the new one will be faded in.

Crossfade() receives an animationSpec of type FiniteAnimationSpec<Float>. It defaults to tween(). This function returns a TweenSpec instance configured with the given duration, delay, and easing curve. The parameters default to DefaultDurationMillis (300 ms), 0, and FastOutSlowInEasing. The easing curve is represented by instances of CubicBezierEasing. This class models third-order Bézier curves. Its constructor receives four parameters:

- The *x* and *y* coordinates of the first control point
- The *x* and *y* coordinates of the second control point

The documentation explains that the line through the point (0, 0) and the first control point is tangent to the easing at the point (0, 0), and that the line through the point (1, 1) and the second control point is tangent to the easing at the point (1, 1). CubicBezierEasing is an implementation of the Easing interface (the androidx. compose.animation.core package). Besides FastOutSlowInEasing, you can choose from three other predefined curves: LinearOutSlowInEasing, FastOutLinearInEasing, and LinearEasing to customize your animation.

As Crossfade() receives an animationSpec of type FiniteAnimationSpec<Float>, you can, for example, pass the following code to use a spring animation with very low stiffness:

```
animationSpec = spring(stiffness = Spring.StiffnessVeryLow)
```

In the next section, we look at how the different specifications of an animation are related.

Understanding animation specifications

AnimationSpec is the base interface for defining animation specifications. It stores the data type to be animated and the animation configuration. Its only function, vectorize(), creates a VectorizedAnimationSpec instance with the given TwoWayConverter (which converts a given type to and from AnimationVector).

The animation system operates on AnimationVector instances. VectorizedAnimationSpec describes how these vectors should be animated, for example, simply interpolating between the start and end values (as you have seen with TweenSpec), showing no animation at all (SnapSpec), or applying spring physics to produce the motion (SpringSpec).

The FiniteAnimationSpec interface extends AnimationSpec. It is directly implemented by the RepeatableSpec and SpringSpec classes. It overrides vectorize() to return VectorizedFiniteAnimationSpec. Now, FiniteAnimationSpec is the parent of the interface DurationBasedAnimationSpec, which overrides vectorize() to return VectorizedDurationBasedAnimationSpec. Then, DurationBasedAnimationSpec is implemented by the TweenSpec, SnapSpec, and KeyframesSpec classes.

To create a KeyframesSpec instance, you can invoke the keyframes() function and pass an initialization function for the animation. After the duration of the animation, you pass mappings of the animating value at a given amount of time in milliseconds:

```
animationSpec = keyframes {
    durationMillis = 8000
```

```
    0f at 0
    1f at 2000
    0f at 4000
    1f at 6000
}
```

In this example, the animation takes 8 seconds, which is longer than you'd ever practically use, but allows you to observe the changes. If you apply the code snippet to `CrossfadeAnimationDemo()`, you will notice that each letter is visible twice during the course of the animation.

So far, we have looked at finite animations. What if you want an animation to continue forever? Jetpack Compose does this in the `CircularProgressIndicator()` and `LinearProgressIndicator()` composables. `InfiniteRepeatableSpec` repeats the provided animation until it is canceled manually.

When used with transitions or other animation composables, the animation will stop when the composable is removed from the compose tree. `InfiniteRepeatableSpec` implements `AnimationSpec`. The constructor expects two arguments, `animation` and `repeatMode`. The `RepeatMode` enum class defines two values, `Restart` and `Reverse`. The default value for `repeatMode` is `RepeatMode.Restart`, meaning each repeat restarts from the beginning.

You can use `infiniteRepeatable()` to create an `InfiniteRepeatableSpec` instance. My `InfiniteRepeatableDemo()` sample composable (*Figure 8.3*) shows you how to do this:

Figure 8.3 – The AnimationDemo sample showing InfiniteRepeatableDemo()

The composable rotates a text clockwise from 0 to 359 degrees. Then, the animation restarts. `Text()` is centered inside `Box()`:

```
@Composable
fun InfiniteRepeatableDemo() {
  val infiniteTransition = rememberInfiniteTransition()
  val degrees by infiniteTransition.animateFloat(
    initialValue = 0F,
    targetValue = 359F,
    animationSpec = infiniteRepeatable(animation =
                      keyframes {
      durationMillis = 1500
      0F at 0
      359F at 1500
    })
  )
  Box(
    modifier = Modifier.fillMaxSize(),
    contentAlignment = Alignment.Center
  ) {
    Text(text = stringResource(id = R.string.app_name),
    modifier = Modifier.rotate(degrees = degrees))
  }
}
```

To create a potentially infinite animation, you first need to remember an infinite transition using `rememberInfiniteTransition()`. You can then invoke `animateFloat()` on the transition instance. This returns `State<Float>`, which is used with the `rotate()` modifier. `infiniteRepeatable()` is passed to `animateFloat()` as its `animationSpec` parameter. The animation itself is based on keyframes. We need to define only two frames, the first representing the start, and the second representing the end angle.

If you want the text to return to its initial angle rather than rotating continuously, you can change the `repeatMode` parameter to the following:

```
repeatMode = RepeatMode.Reverse
```

Then you should add short delays to the beginning and the end. `keyframes {}` should look like this:

```
keyframes {
    durationMillis = 2000
    0F at 500
    359F at 1500
}
```

This concludes our look at animation specifications. To finish this chapter, let me briefly summarize what you have learned, and what you can expect in the next chapter.

Summary

This chapter showed you how easy it is to use Jetpack Compose to enrich your apps with animations and transitions. We started by using simple animations to visualize state changes. For example, I introduced you to `animateColorAsState()`. We then used `updateTransition()` to obtain `Transition` instances and invoked extension functions such as `animateDp()` and `animateFloat()` to animate several values based on state changes simultaneously.

The *Showing and hiding UI elements with animations* section introduced you to the `AnimatedVisibility()` composable function, which allows you to apply enter and exit transitions. They are played back while the content appears or disappears. You also learned how to animate size changes using the `animateContentSize()` modifier.

In the final main section, *Spicing up transitions through visual effects*, we used the `Crossfade()` composable function to switch between two layouts with a crossfade animation. Furthermore, you learned about `AnimationSpec` and related classes and interfaces. I concluded the section with a take on infinite animations.

In *Chapter 9*, *Exploring Interoperability APIs*, you will learn how to mix old-fashioned views and composable functions. We will once again return to ViewModels as a means for sharing data between both worlds. And I will show you how to integrate third-party libraries in your Compose app.

9
Exploring Interoperability APIs

The aim of this book is to show you how to develop beautiful, fast, and maintainable Jetpack Compose apps. The previous chapters helped you get familiar with core techniques and principles, as well as important interfaces, classes, packages, and—of course—composable functions. The remaining chapters cover topics beyond a successful adoption of Android's new declarative user interface toolkit.

In this chapter, we are going to look at `AndroidView()`, `AndroidViewBinding()`, and `ComposeView` as the interoperability **application programming interfaces (APIs)** of Jetpack Compose. The main sections are listed here:

- Showing Views in a Compose app

- Sharing data between Views and composable functions

- Embedding composables in View hierarchies

We start by looking at how to show a traditional View hierarchy in a Compose app. Imagine you have written a custom component (which under the hood consists of several UI elements), such as an image picker, a color chooser, or a camera preview. Instead of rewriting your component with Jetpack Compose, you can save your investment by simply reusing it. A lot of third-party libraries are still written in Views, so I will show you how to use them in Compose apps.

Once you have embedded a View in a Compose app, you need to share data between the View and your composable functions. The *Sharing data between Views and composable functions* section explains how to do this with ViewModels.

Often, you may not want to rewrite an app from scratch but migrate it to Jetpack Compose gradually, replacing View hierarchies with composable functions step by step. The final main section, *Embedding composables in View hierarchies*, discusses how to include a Compose hierarchy in existing View-based apps.

Technical requirements

This chapter is based on the `ZxingDemo` and `InteropDemo` samples. Please refer to the *Technical requirements* section of *Chapter 1, Building Your First Compose App*, for information about how to install and set up Android Studio, and how to get the repository accompanying this book.

All the code files for this chapter can be found on GitHub at `https://github.com/PacktPublishing/Android-UI-Development-with-Jetpack-Compose/tree/main/chapter_09`.

Showing Views in a Compose app

Imagine you have written a View-based custom component for one of your previous apps—for example, an image picker, a color chooser, or a camera preview—or you would like to include a third-party library such as *Zebra Crossing (ZXing)* to scan **Quick Response (QR)** codes and barcodes. To incorporate them into a Compose app, you need to add the View (or the root of a View hierarchy) to your composable functions.

Let's see how this works.

Adding custom components to a Compose app

The `ZxingDemo` sample, shown in the following screenshot, uses the *ZXing Android Embedded* barcode scanner library for Android, which is based on the ZXing decoder. It is released under the terms of the Apache License 2.0 and is hosted on GitHub (`https://github.com/journeyapps/zxing-android-embedded`):

Figure 9.1 – The ZxingDemo sample

My example continuously scans for barcodes and QR codes. The decorated barcode view is provided by the library. If the scanner engine provides a result, the corresponding text is shown as an overlay using `Text()`. To use *ZXing Android Embedded*, you need to add an implementation dependency to your module-level `build.gradle` file, as follows:

```
implementation 'com.journeyapps:zxing-android-embedded:4.3.0'
```

The scanner accesses the camera and (optionally) the device vibrator. The app must request at least `android.permission.WAKE_LOCK` and `android.permission.CAMERA` permissions in the manifest, and the `android.permission.CAMERA` permission during runtime. My implementation is based on `ActivityResultContracts.RequestPermission`, which replaces the traditional approach overriding `onRequestPermissionsResult()`. Also, depending on the lifecycle of the activity, the scanner must be paused and resumed. For the sake of simplicity, I use a `lateinit` variable named `barcodeView` and invoke `barcodeView.pause()` and `barcodeView.resume()` when needed. Please refer to the source code of the project for details. Next, I will show you how to initialize the scanner library. This involves inflating a layout file (named `layout.xml`), as follows:

```
<?xml version="1.0" encoding="utf-8"?>
<com.journeyapps.barcodescanner.DecoratedBarcodeView
  xmlns:android="http://schemas.android.com/apk/res/android"
```

```
android:id="@+id/barcode_scanner"
android:layout_width="match_parent"
android:layout_height="match_parent"
android:layout_alignParentTop="true" />
```

The layout consists of only one element, DecoratedBarcodeView. It is configured to fill all available space. The following code snippet is part of onCreate(). Please remember that barcodeView is accessed in some lifecycle functions such as onPause(), and therefore is a lateinit property:

```
val root = layoutInflater.inflate(R.layout.layout, null)
barcodeView = root.findViewById(R.id.barcode_scanner)
val formats = listOf(BarcodeFormat.QR_CODE,
    BarcodeFormat.CODE_39)
barcodeView.barcodeView.decoderFactory =
    DefaultDecoderFactory(formats)
barcodeView.initializeFromIntent(intent)
val callback = object : BarcodeCallback {
  override fun barcodeResult(result: BarcodeResult) {
    if (result.text == null || result.text == text.value) {
      return
    }
    text.value = result.text
  }
}
barcodeView.decodeContinuous(callback)
```

First, layout.xml is inflated and assigned to root. Then, barcodeView is initialized (initializeFromIntent()) and configured (by setting a decoder factory). Finally, the continuous scanning process is started using decodeContinuous(). The callback lambda expression is invoked every time a new scan result is available. The text variable is defined like this:

```
private val text = MutableLiveData("")
```

I am using MutableLiveData, because it can easily be observed as state. Before I show you how to access it inside a composable function, let's briefly recap, as follows:

- We have set up and activated the scanner library.

- When it detects a barcode or a QR code, it updates the value of a
  `MutableLiveData` instance.

- We defined and initialized two `View` instances—`root` and `barcodeView`.

Next, I show you how to access the state obtained from the ViewModel inside a composable, as follows:

```
setContent {
    val state = text.observeAsState()
    state.value?.let {
        ZxingDemo(root, it)
    }
}
```

The value of the state and `root` are passed to the `ZxingDemo()` composable. We display `value` using `Text()`. The `root` parameter is used to include the View hierarchy in the Compose UI. The code is illustrated in the following snippet:

```
@Composable
fun ZxingDemo(root: View, value: String) {
    Box(
        modifier = Modifier.fillMaxSize(),
        contentAlignment = Alignment.TopCenter
    ) {
        AndroidView(modifier = Modifier.fillMaxSize(),
            factory = {
                root
            })
        if (value.isNotBlank()) {
            Text(
                modifier = Modifier.padding(16.dp),
                text = value,
                color = Color.White,
                style = MaterialTheme.typography.h4
            )
        }
    }
}
```

The UI consists of a `Box()` composable with two children, `AndroidView()` and `Text()`. `AndroidView()` receives a `factory` block, which just returns `root` (the View hierarchy containing the scanner viewfinder). The `Text()` composable shows the last scan result.

The `factory` block is called exactly once, to obtain the View to be composed. It will always be invoked on the UI thread, so you can set View properties as needed. In my example, this is not needed, as all initialization has already been done in `onCreate()`. Configuring the barcode scanner should not be done in a composable, because preparing the camera and preview is potentially time-consuming. Also, parts of the component tree are accessed on the activity level, therefore references to children (`barcodeView`) are needed anyway.

In this section, I have shown you how to include a View hierarchy in your Compose app using `AndroidView()`. This composable function is one of the important pieces of the Jetpack Compose interoperability APIs. We used `layoutInflater.inflate()` to inflate the component tree and `findViewById()` to access one of its children. Modern View-based apps try to avoid `findViewById()` and use *View Binding* instead. In the next section, you will learn how to combine View Binding and composable functions.

Inflating View hierarchies with AndroidViewBinding()

Traditionally, activities held references to Views in `lateinit` properties, if the corresponding components needed to be modified in different functions. The *Inflating layout files* section of *Chapter 2, Understanding the Declarative Paradigm*, discussed some of the issues with this approach and introduced View Binding as a solution. It was adopted by many apps. Therefore, if you want to migrate an existing app to Jetpack Compose, you likely need to combine View Binding and composable functions. This section explains how to achieve that.

The following screenshot shows the `InteropDemo` sample:

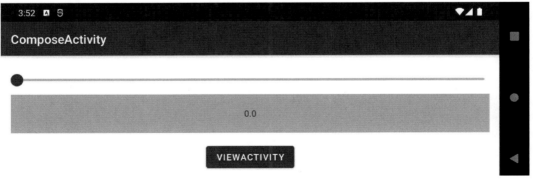

Figure 9.2 – The InteropDemo sample

The `InteropDemo` sample consists of two activities. One (`ViewActivity`) integrates a composable function in a `View` hierarchy. We will turn to this in the *Embedding composables in View hierarchies* section. The second one, `ComposeActivity`, does the opposite: it inflates a `View` hierarchy using View Binding and shows the component tree inside a `Column()` composable. Let's take a look here:

```
class ComposeActivity : ComponentActivity() {
  override fun onCreate(savedInstanceState: Bundle?) {
    super.onCreate(savedInstanceState)
    val viewModel: MyViewModel by viewModels()
    ...
    setContent {
      ViewIntegrationDemo(viewModel) {
        val i = Intent(
          this,
          ViewActivity::class.java
        )
        i.putExtra(KEY, viewModel.sliderValue.value)
        startActivity(i)
      }
    }
  }
}
```

The root composable is called `ViewIntegrationDemo()`. It receives a ViewModel and a lambda expression. The ViewModel is used to share data between the Compose and the `View` hierarchies, which I will discuss in the *Sharing data between Views and composable functions* section. The lambda expression starts `ViewActivity` and passes a value from the ViewModel (`sliderValue`). The code is illustrated in the following snippet:

```
@Composable
fun ViewIntegrationDemo(viewModel: MyViewModel,
                        onClick: () -> Unit) {
  val sliderValueState =
    viewModel.sliderValue.observeAsState()
  Scaffold( ... ) {
    Column( ... ) {
      Slider( … )
```

```
AndroidViewBinding(
    modifier = Modifier.fillMaxWidth(),
    factory = CustomBinding::inflate
) {
    // Here Views will be updated
}
}
}
}
```

`Scaffold()` is an important integrational composable function. It structures a Compose screen. Besides top and bottom bars, it contains some content—in this case, a `Column()` composable with two children, `Slider()` and `AndroidViewBinding()`. The slider gets its current value from a ViewModel and propagates changes back to it. You will learn more about that in the *Revisiting ViewModels* section.

`AndroidViewBinding()` is similar to `AndroidView()`. A `factory` block creates a View hierarchy to be composed. `CustomBinding::inflate` inflates the layout from the `custom.xml` file represented by `CustomBinding` and returns an instance of this type. The class is created and updated during builds. It provides constants that reflect the contents of a layout file named `custom.xml`. Here is an abridged version:

```xml
<?xml version="1.0" encoding="utf-8"?>
<androidx.constraintlayout.widget.ConstraintLayout
    xmlns:android="http://schemas.android.com/apk/res/android"
    xmlns:app="http://schemas.android.com/apk/res-auto"
    android:layout_width="match_parent"
    android:layout_height="match_parent">

    <com.google.android.material.textview.MaterialTextView
        android:id="@+id/textView"
        ... />

    <com.google.android.material.button.MaterialButton
        android:id="@+id/button"
        ...
```

```
        android:text="@string/view_activity"
        ...
        app:layout_constraintTop_toBottomOf="@id/textView" />

</androidx.constraintlayout.widget.ConstraintLayout>
```

This `ConstraintLayout` has two children, a `MaterialTextView` and a `MaterialButton`. A button click invokes the lambda expression passed to `ViewIntegrationDemo()`. The text fields receive the current slider value. This is done in the update block. The following code belongs below `// Here Views will be updated` inside `ViewIntegrationDemo()`:

```
textView.text = sliderValueState.value.toString()
button.setOnClickListener {
    onClick()
}
```

You may be wondering where `textView` and `button` are defined, and why they can be accessed immediately. The `update` block is invoked right after the layout is inflated. It is an extension function of the type whose instance is returned by `inflate`—in my example, `CustomBinding`. Because the **identifiers (IDs)** of the button and the text field in `custom.xml` are `button` and `textView`, there are corresponding variables in `CustomBinding`.

The `update` block is also invoked when a value being used by it (`sliderValueState.value`) changes. In the next section, we look at when and where such changes are triggered.

Sharing data between Views and composable functions

State is app data that may change over time. Recomposition occurs when state being used by a composable changes. To achieve something similar in the traditional View world, we need to store data in a way that changes to it can be observed. There are many implementations of the *Observable* pattern. The Android Architecture Components (and subsequent Jetpack versions) include `LiveData` and `MutableLiveData`. Both are frequently used inside ViewModels to store state outside activities.

Revisiting ViewModels

I introduced you to ViewModels in the *Surviving configuration changes* section of *Chapter 5, Managing the State of Your Composable Functions*, and the *Persisting and retrieving state* section of *Chapter 7, Tips, Tricks, and Best Practices*. Before we look at how to use ViewModels to synchronize data between Views and composable functions, let's briefly recap on key techniques, as follows:

- To create or get an instance of a ViewModel, use the top-level `viewModels()` function, which belongs to the `androidx.activity` package.

- To observe `LiveData` instances as compose state, invoke the `observeAsState()` extension function on a ViewModel property inside a composable function.

- To observe `LiveData` instances outside of composable functions, invoke `observe()`. This function belongs to `androidx.lifecycle.LiveData`.

- To change a ViewModel property, invoke the corresponding setter.

> **Important Note**
>
> Please make sure to add implementation dependencies of `androidx.compose.runtime:runtime-livedata`, `androidx.lifecycle:lifecycle-runtime-ktx`, and `androidx.lifecycle:lifecycle-viewmodel-compose` in the module-level `build.gradle` file as needed.

Now that we have refamiliarized ourselves with key techniques related to ViewModels, let's look at how the synchronization between Views and composable functions works. *Synchronization* means that a composable function and code related to a View observe the same ViewModel property and may trigger changes on that property. Triggering changes is usually done by invoking a setter. For a `Slider()` composable, it may look like this:

```
Slider(
  modifier = Modifier.fillMaxWidth(),
  onValueChange = {
    viewModel.setSliderValue(it)
  },
  value = sliderValueState.value ?: 0F
)
```

This example also shows the readout inside a composable (`sliderValueState.value`). Here is how `sliderValueState` has been defined:

```
val sliderValueState = viewModel.sliderValue.observeAsState()
```

Next, let's look at traditional (non-Compose) code using View Binding. The following examples are part of `ViewActivity`, which also belongs to the `InteropDemo` sample.

Combining View Binding and ViewModels

Activities taking advantage of View Binding usually have a `lateinit` property named `binding`, as illustrated in the following code snippet:

```
binding = LayoutBinding.inflate(layoutInflater)
```

`LayoutBinding.inflate()` returns an instance of `LayoutBinding`. `Binding.root` represents the root of the component tree. It is passed to `setContentView()`. Here is an abridged version of the corresponding layout file (`layout.xml`):

```xml
<?xml version="1.0" encoding="utf-8"?>
<androidx.constraintlayout.widget.ConstraintLayout
  xmlns:android="http://schemas.android.com/apk/res/android"
  ...
  android:layout_width="match_parent"
  android:layout_height="match_parent">

  <com.google.android.material.slider.Slider
    android:id="@+id/slider"
    ... />

  <androidx.compose.ui.platform.ComposeView
    android:id="@+id/compose_view"
    ...
    app:layout_constraintTop_toBottomOf="@id/slider" />

</androidx.constraintlayout.widget.ConstraintLayout>
```

ConstraintLayout contains a com.google.android.material.slider.
Slider and a ComposeView (which is discussed in detail in the following section).
The ID of the slider is slider, so LayoutBinding contains an equally named variable.
We can therefore link the slider to the ViewModel, like this:

```
viewModel.sliderValue.observe(this) {
    binding.slider.value = it
}
```

The block passed to observe() is invoked when the value stored in sliderValue
changes. By updating binding.slider.value, we change the position of the slider
handle, which means we update the slider. The code is illustrated here:

```
binding.slider.addOnChangeListener { _, value, _ ->
    viewModel.setSliderValue(value) }
```

The block passed to addOnChangeListener() is invoked when the user drags the
slider handle. By invoking setSliderValue() we update the ViewModel, which in
turn triggers updates on observers—for example, our composable functions.

In this section, I familiarized you with the steps needed to tie composable functions and
traditional Views to a ViewModel property. When the property is changed, all observers
are called, which leads to the update of both the composable and View. In the following
section, we continue our look at the InteropDemo sample. This time, I will show
you how to embed composables in a View hierarchy. This is important if an existing app is
to be migrated to Jetpack Compose step by step.

Embedding composables in View hierarchies

As you have seen, integrating Views in composable functions is simple and
straightforward using AndroidView() and AndroidViewBinding(). But what
about the other way round? Often, you may not want to rewrite an existing (View-based)
app from scratch but migrate it to Jetpack Compose gradually, replacing View hierarchies
with composable functions step by step. Depending on the complexity of the activity,
it may make sense to start with small composables that reflect portions of the UI and
incorporate them into the remaining layout.

`Androidx.compose.ui.platform.ComposeView` makes composables available inside classic layouts. The class extends `AbstractComposeView`, which has `ViewGroup` as its parent. Once the layout that includes the ComposeView has been inflated, here is how you configure it:

```
binding.composeView.run {
  setViewCompositionStrategy(
      ViewCompositionStrategy.DisposeOnDetachedFromWindow)
  setContent {
    val sliderValue =
            viewModel.sliderValue.observeAsState()
    sliderValue.value?.let {
      ComposeDemo(it) {
        val I = Intent(
          context,
          ComposeActivity::class.java
        )
        i.putExtra(KEY, it)
        startActivity(i)
      }
    }
  }
}
```

`setContent()` sets the content for this view. An initial composition will occur when the view is attached to a window, or when `createComposition()` is called. While `setContent()` is defined in `ComposeView`, `createComposition()` belongs to `AbstractComposeView`. It performs the initial composition for this view. Typically, you do not need to invoke this function directly.

`setViewCompositionStrategy()` configures how to manage the disposal of the View's internal composition. `ViewCompositionStrategy.DisposeOnDetached FromWindow` (the default) means that the composition is disposed whenever the view becomes detached from a window. This is preferred for simple scenarios, as in my example. If your view is shown inside a fragment or a component with a known `LifecycleOwner`, you should use `DisposeOnViewTreeLifecycleDestroyed` or `DisposeOnLifecycleDestroyed` instead. These, however, are topics beyond the scope of this book. The following line creates state based on the `sliderValue` property of the ViewModel and passes the value to `ComposeDemo()`:

```
val sliderValue = viewModel.sliderValue.observeAsState()
```

This composable also receives a block that launches `ComposeActivity` and passes the current slider value to it, as illustrated in the following code snippet:

```
@Composable
fun ComposeDemo(value: Float, onClick: () -> Unit) {
  Column(
    modifier = Modifier
      .fillMaxSize(),
    horizontalAlignment = Alignment.CenterHorizontally
  ) {
    Box(
      modifier = Modifier
        .fillMaxWidth()
        .background(MaterialTheme.colors.secondary)
        .height(64.dp),
      contentAlignment = Alignment.Center
    ) {
      Text(
        text = value.toString()
      )
    }
    Button(
      onClick = onClick,
      modifier = Modifier.padding(top = 16.dp)
    ) {
      Text(text = stringResource(id =
            R.string.compose_activity))
    }
  }
}
```

`ComposeDemo()`, as illustrated in the following screenshot, puts a `Box()` (which contains a `Text()`) and a `Button()` inside a `Column()`, in order to resemble `ViewActivity`. Wrapping `Text()` inside the `Box()` is necessary to vertically center the text inside an area with a particular height. A click on the button invokes the `onClick` lambda expression. `Text()` just shows the `value` parameter:

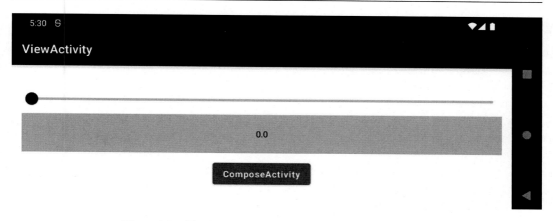

Figure 9.3 – The InteropDemo sample showing ViewActivity

Before closing out this chapter, let me recap on important steps you need to take to include a Compose hierarchy in a layout, as follows:

- Add `androidx.compose.ui.platform.ComposeView` to the layout.

- Decide on a `ViewCompositionStrategy`, depending on where the layout is shown (activity, fragment, …).

- Set the content using `setContent {}`.

- Obtain a reference to the `ViewModel` by invoking `viewModels()`.

- Register listeners to relevant Views and update the `ViewModel` upon changes.

- Inside composable functions, create state by invoking `observeAsState()` on ViewModel properties as needed.

- Inside composables, update the ViewModel by invoking corresponding setters.

Jetpack Compose interoperability APIs allow for seamless two-way integration of composable functions and `View` hierarchies. They help you use libraries that rely on Views and ease the transition to Compose by making a gradual, fine-grained migration possible.

Summary

In this chapter, we looked at the interoperability APIs of Jetpack Compose, which allow you to mix composable functions and traditional Views. We started by incorporating a traditional View hierarchy from a third-party library in a Compose app, using `AndroidView()`. As recent apps favor View Binding over the direct use of `findViewById()`, I also showed you how to embed layouts in a composable with View Binding and `AndroidViewBinding()`. Once you have embedded a `View` in a Compose UI, you need to share data between the two worlds. The *Sharing data between Views and composable functions* section explained how to achieve this with ViewModels. The final main section, *Embedding composables in View hierarchies*, discussed how to include a Compose UI in existing apps using `ComposeView`.

Chapter 10, Testing and Debugging Compose Apps, focuses on testing your Compose apps. You will learn how to use `ComposeTestRule` and `AndroidComposeTestRule`. Also, I will introduce you to the *semantics tree*.

10
Testing and Debugging Compose Apps

Programming is a very creative process. Implementing great-looking **user interfaces (UIs)** with slick animations is pure fun with Jetpack Compose. However, making an outstanding app involves more than just writing code. Testing and debugging are equally as important because no matter how carefully you design and implement your app, bugs and glitches are inevitable, at least in non-trivial programs. Yet there is nothing to fear, as there are powerful tools you can wield to check if your code is acting as intended.

This chapter introduces you to these tools. Its main sections are listed here:

- Setting up and writing tests
- Understanding semantics
- Debugging Compose apps

In the first main section, I will walk you through important terms and techniques regarding testing. We will set up the infrastructure, write a simple unit test, and then turn to Compose specifics—for example, `createComposeRule()` and `createAndroidComposeRule()`.

The *Understanding semantics* section builds on these foundations. We look at how composable functions are selected—or found—in a test, and why making your app accessible also helps to write better tests. You will also learn about actions and assertions.

Failing tests often hint at bugs unless, of course, the failure is intentional. If you suspect the code being checked by a test is buggy, a debugging session is due. The final main section, *Debugging Compose apps*, explains how to examine your Compose code. We will be revisiting the semantics tree, discussed in the *Understanding semantics* section. Finally, I will show you how to take advantage of `InspectorInfo` and `InspectorValueInfo`.

Technical requirements

This chapter is based on the `TestingAndDebuggingDemo` sample. Please refer to *Technical requirements* section of *Chapter 1, Building Your First Compose App*, for information about how to install and set up Android Studio and how to get the repository accompanying this book.

All the code files for this chapter can be found on GitHub at `https://github.com/PacktPublishing/Android-UI-Development-with-Jetpack-Compose/tree/main/chapter_10`.

Setting up and writing tests

As a software developer, you probably enjoy writing code. Seeing an app gain functionality feels very rewarding, probably more than writing tests—or worse, finding bugs—yet testing and debugging are essential. Eventually, your code will contain bugs, because all non-trivial programs do. To make your developer life easier, you need to familiarize yourself with writing tests and with debugging your own and others' code. Testing an app has various facets that correspond to different types of tests, as outlined here:

- **Unit test**: You need to make sure that the business logic works as expected. This, for example, means that formulae and calculations always produce correct results.

- **Integration tests**: Are all building blocks of the app properly integrated? Depending on what the app does, this may include accessing remote services, talking to a database, or reading and writing files on the device.

- **UI tests**: Is the UI accurate? Are all UI elements visible on all supported screen sizes? Do they always show the right values? Do interactions such as button clicks or slider movements trigger the intended function? And something very important: are all parts of the app accessible?

The number of tests varies among types. It has long been claimed that, ideally, most of your tests should be unit tests, followed by integration tests. This leads to the perception of a **test pyramid**, with unit tests being its foundation and UI tests the tip. As with all metaphors, the test pyramid has seen both support and harsh criticism. If you want to learn more about it, and testing strategies in general, please refer to the *Further reading* section at the end of this chapter. Jetpack Compose tests are UI tests. So, while you likely write many corresponding test cases, testing the underlying business logic using unit tests may well be even more important.

To make testing reliable, comprehensible, and reproducible, automation is used. In the next section, I will show you how to write unit tests using the *JUnit 4* testing framework.

Implementing unit tests

Units are small, isolated pieces of code—usually a function, method, subroutine, or property, depending on the programming language. Let's look at a simple Kotlin function in the following code snippet:

```
fun isEven(num: Int): Boolean {
    val div2 = num / 2
    return (div2 * 2) == num
}
```

isEven() determines if the passed Int value is even. If this is the case, the function returns true; otherwise, it returns false. The algorithm is based on the fact that only even Int values can be divided by 2 without a remainder. Assuming we use the function often, we certainly want to make sure that the result is always correct. But how do we do that (how do we test that)? To verify isEven() exhaustively, we would need to check every possible input value, ranging from Int.MIN_VALUE to Int.MAX_VALUE. Even on fast computers, this may take some time. Part of the art of writing good unit tests is to identify all the important boundaries and transitions. Regarding isEven(), these might be the following ones:

- Int.MIN_VALUE and Int.MAX_VALUE
- One negative even and one negative odd Int value
- One positive even and one positive odd Int value

To write and execute unit tests, you should add the following dependencies to your module-level `build.gradle` properties file:

```
androidTestImplementation "androidx.test.ext:junit:1.1.3"
androidTestImplementation "androidx.compose.ui:ui-test-
   junit4:$compose_version"
debugImplementation "androidx.compose.ui:ui-test-
   manifest:$compose_version"
testImplementation 'junit:junit:4.13.2'
androidTestImplementation "androidx.test.espresso:espresso-
   core:3.4.0"
```

Depending on which types of tests you will be adding to your app project, some of the preceding dependencies will be optional. For example, `androidx.test.espresso` is needed only if your app also contains old-fashioned Views you wish to test (such as in interoperability scenarios).

Unit tests are executed on your development machine. Test classes are placed inside the `app/src/test/java` directory and are available through the **Project** tool window, as illustrated in the following screenshot. The Android Studio project assistant configures your projects accordingly and creates a test class, which I have renamed `SimpleUnitTest`:

Figure 10.1 – Unit tests in the Android Studio Project tool window

Let's look at the class in the following code snippet:

```
Package
   eu.thomaskuenneth.composebook.testinganddebuggingdemo
```

```kotlin
import org.junit.*
import org.junit.Assert.assertEquals

class SimpleUnitTest {
  companion object {
    @BeforeClass
    @JvmStatic
    fun setupAll() {
      println("Setting things up")
    }
  }

  @Before
  fun setup() {
    println("Setup test")
  }

  @After
  fun teardown() {
    println("Clean up test")
  }

  @Test
  fun testListOfInts() {
    val nums = listOf(Int.MIN_VALUE, -3, -2, 2, 3,
                      Int.MAX_VALUE)
    val results = listOf(true, false, true, true, false,
                      false)
    nums.forEachIndexed { index, num ->
      val result = isEven(num)
      println("isEven($num) returns $result")
      assertEquals(result, results[index])
    }
  }
}
```

A test class contains one or more tests. A **test** (also called a **test case**) is an ordinary Kotlin function, annotated with `@Test`. It checks certain well-defined situations, conditions, or criteria. Tests should be isolated, which means they should not rely on previous ones. My example tests if `isEven()` returns correct results for six input values. Such checks are based on **assertions**. An assertion formulates expected behavior. If an assertion is not met, the test fails.

If you need something to be done before or after each test, you can implement functions and annotate them with `@Before` or `@After`. You can achieve something similar using `@Rule`. We will be looking at this in the following section. To run code before all tests, you need to implement a companion object with a function annotated with `@BeforeClass` and `@JvmStatic`. `@AfterClass` is useful for cleanup purposes after all tests have been run.

You can run a unit test by right-clicking on the test class in the **Project** tool window and choosing **Run '...'**. Once a launch configuration for the test class has been created, you can also run the tests using the menu bar and the toolbar. Test results are presented in the **Run** tool window, as illustrated in the following screenshot:

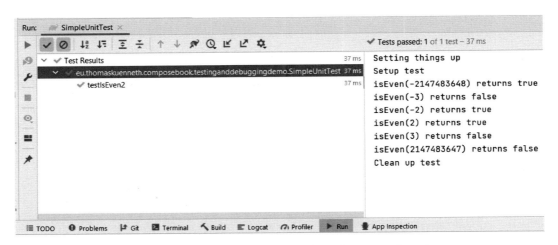

Figure 10.2 – Test results in the Android Studio Run tool window

Although the test passes, my implementation of `isEven()` may still not be flawless. While the test checks the upper and lower bounds, it leaves the transition between negative and positive numbers untested. Let's correct this and add another test, as follows:

```kotlin
@Test
fun testIsEvenZero() {
    assertEquals(true, isEven(0))
}
```

Fortunately, this test passes, too.

> **Important Note**
> Pay close attention to the parameters a unit receives and the result it produces.
> Always test boundaries and transitions. Make sure to cover all code paths (if
> possible) and watch for pitfalls such as exceptions due to invalid arguments (for
> example, division by zero or wrong number formats).

Please remember that composable functions are top-level Kotlin functions, so they are
prime candidates for unit tests. Let's see how this works. In the next section, you will learn
to test a simple Compose UI.

Testing composable functions

The `SimpleButtonDemo()` composable (which belongs to the
`TestingAndDebuggingDemo` sample) shows a box with a button centered inside.
Clicking the button for the first time changes its text from **A** to **B**. Subsequent clicks toggle
between **B** and **A**. The code is illustrated in the following snippet:

```
@Composable
fun SimpleButtonDemo() {
  val a = stringResource(id = R.string.a)
  val b = stringResource(id = R.string.b)
  var text by remember { mutableStateOf(a) }
  Box(
    modifier = Modifier.fillMaxSize(),
    contentAlignment = Alignment.Center
  ) {
    Button(onClick = {
      text = if (text == a) b else a
    }) {
      Text(text = text)
    }
  }
}
```

The text is stored as a mutable `String` state. It is changed inside the `onClick` block and used as a parameter for the `Text()` composable. If we want to test `SimpleButtonDemo()`, some aspects we likely need to check are these:

- **Initial state of the UI**: Is the initial button text **A**?

- **Behavior**: Does the first button click change the text to **B**?

    Do subsequent clicks toggle between **B** and **A**?

Here's what a simple test class looks like:

```kotlin
@RunWith(AndroidJUnit4::class)
class SimpleInstrumentedTest {

  @get:Rule
  val rule = createComposeRule()

  @Before
  fun setup() {
    rule.setContent {
      SimpleButtonDemo()
    }
  }

  @Test
  fun testInitialLetterIsA() {
    rule.onNodeWithText("A").assertExists()
  }
}
```

Unlike the `SimpleUnitTest` class from the *Implementing unit tests* section, its source code is stored inside the `app/src/androidTest/java` directory (contrary to `.../test/...` for ordinary unit tests). `SimpleInstrumentedTest` is an **instrumented test**. Contrary to plain unit tests, they are not executed locally on the development machine, but on the Android Emulator or a real device, because they need Android-specific functionality to run. Instrumented tests are available through the **Project** tool window, as illustrated in the following screenshot:

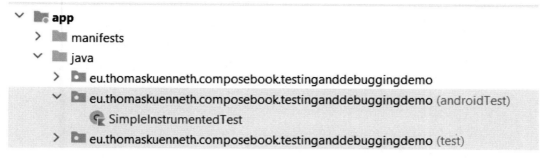

Figure 10.3 – Instrumented tests in the Android Studio Project tool window

You can run an instrumented test by right-clicking on the test class in the **Project** tool window and choosing **Run '…'**. Once a launch configuration for the test class has been created, you can also run the tests using the menu bar and the toolbar. Test results are presented in the **Run** tool window, as illustrated in the following screenshot:

Figure 10.4 – Instrumented test results in the Android Studio Run tool window

JUnit **rules** allow you to run some code alongside a test case. In a way, this is like having @Before and @After annotations in your test class. There are several predefined rules—for example, the TestName rule can provide the current test name inside a test method, as follows:

```
@get:Rule
var name = TestName()

...

@Test
fun testPrintMethodName() {
    println(name.methodName)
}
```

When the testPrintMethodName() function runs, it prints its name. You can see the output in **Logcat**. Please remember—you need to apply the @Rule annotation to the property getter by adding get:. Failing to do so will result in a ValidationError (The @Rule '…' must be public) message during execution.

Compose tests are based on rules. `createComposeRule()` returns an implementation of the `ComposeContentTestRule` interface, which extends `ComposeTestRule`. This interface in turn extends `org.junit.rules.TestRule`. Each `TestRule` instance implements `apply()`. This method receives `Statement` and returns the same, a modified, or completely new `Statement`. However, writing your own test rules is beyond the scope of this book. To learn more, please refer to the *Further reading* section at the end of this chapter.

Which implementation of the `ComposeContentTestRule` interface `createComposeRule()` returns depends on the platform. It is `AndroidComposeTestRule<ComponentActivity>` on Android. That is why you should add a dependency to `androidx.compose.ui:ui-test-manifest` in the module-level `build.gradle` file. Otherwise, you may need to manually add a reference to `ComponentActivity` in the manifest file.

`createAndroidComposeRule()` allows you to create `AndroidComposeTestRule` for activity classes other than `ComponentActivity`. This is useful if you require the functionality of this activity in a test. On Compose for Desktop or Web, `createComposeRule()` may return different implementations of `ComposeContentTestRule`, depending on where the Compose UI is hosted. To help make your tests platform-independent, use `createComposeRule()` whenever possible.

Your test cases use (among others) methods provided by `ComposeContentTestRule` implementations. For example, `setContent()` sets the composable function to act as the content of the current screen—that is, the UI to be tested. `setContent()` should be called exactly once per test. To achieve this, just invoke it in a function annotated with `@Before`.

Important Note

If you want to reuse your tests among platforms, try to rely only on methods defined in the `ComposeContentTestRule`, `ComposeContentTestRule`, and `TestRule` interfaces. Avoid calling functions from the implementation.

Next, let's look at `testInitialLetterIsA()`. This test case checks if the initial button text is **A**. To do so, the test must find the button, get its text, and compare it to `"A"`. This comparison is done with an `assertExists()` **assertion**. `onNodeWithText()` is called a **finder**. Finders work on **semantics nodes**, and you will learn more about these in the *Understanding semantics* section. But first: why do we need to *find* the composable to be tested anyway?

Unlike the traditional View system, Jetpack Compose does not use references to identify individual UI elements. Please remember that such references are needed in an imperative approach to modify the component tree during runtime. But this is not how Compose works—instead, we declare how the UI should look based on state. Yet, to test if a particular composable looks and behaves as expected, we need to find it among all other children of a Compose hierarchy.

This is where the **semantics tree** comes into play. As the name implies, *semantics* give meaning to a UI element or element hierarchies. The semantics tree is generated alongside the UI hierarchy, which it describes using attributes such as `Role`, `Text`, and `Actions`. It is used for accessibility and testing.

Before we move on, let's briefly recap: `onNodeWithText()` tries to find a composable (to be, more precisely, a semantics node) with a given text. `assertExists()` checks if a matching node is present in the current UI. If so, the test passes. Otherwise, it fails.

Understanding semantics

In the previous section, I showed you a simple test case that checks if a button text matches a given string. Here is another test case. It performs a click on the button to see if the button text changes as expected:

```
@Test
fun testLetterAfterButtonClickIsB() {
   rule.onNodeWithText("A")
      .performClick()
      .assert(hasText("B"))
}
```

Again, we start by finding the button. `performClick()` (this is called an **action**) clicks it. `Assert(hasText("B"))` checks if the button text is **B** afterward. Assertions determine if a test passes or fails.

`onNodeWithText()` (an extension function of `SemanticsNodeInteractions Provider`) returns a `SemanticsNodeInteraction` semantics node. The `SemanticsNodeInteractionsProvider` interface is the main entry point into testing and is typically implemented by a test rule. It defines two methods, as follows:

- `onNode()` finds and returns a semantics node (`SemanticsNodeInteraction`) that matches the given condition.

- `onAllNodes()` finds all semantics nodes that match the given condition. It returns a `SemanticsNodeInteractionCollection` instance.

Both are called **finders** because they return (*find*) semantics nodes matching certain conditions.

Working with semantics nodes

To see what the semantics node we tested with `testLetterAfterButtonClickIsB()` from the previous section looks like, you can add the following expression after `.assert(…)`:

```
.printToLog("SimpleInstrumentedTest")
```

The result is visible in **Logcat**, as illustrated in the following screenshot:

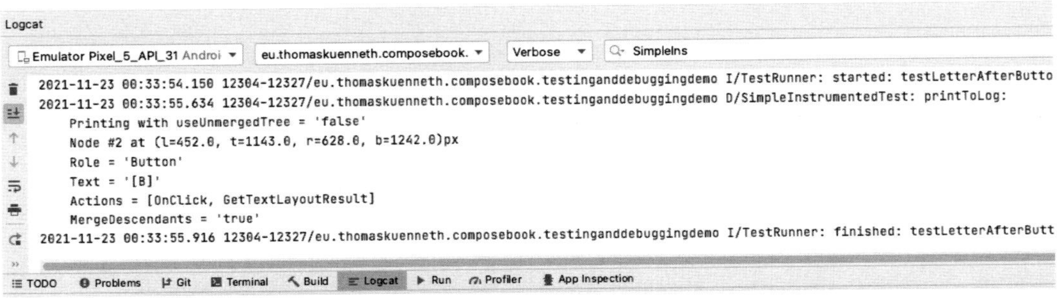

Figure 10.5 – A semantics node in Logcat

`SemanticsNodeInteraction` represents a semantics node. You can interact with a node by performing actions such as `performClick()` or assertions such as `assertHasClickAction()`, or you can navigate to other nodes such as `onChildren()`. Such functions are extension functions of `SemanticsNodeInteraction`. `SemanticsNodeInteractionCollection` is a collection of semantics nodes.

Let's look at another finder function, `onNodeWithContentDescription()`. We will be using it to test if `Image()` is part of the current UI. The code is illustrated in the following snippet:

```
@Composable
fun ImageDemo() {
  Image(
    painter = painterResource(id =
        R.drawable.ic_baseline_airport_shuttle_24),
    contentDescription = stringResource(id =
        R.string.airport_shuttle),
```

```
      contentScale = ContentScale.FillBounds,
      modifier = Modifier
          .size(width = 128.dp, height = 128.dp)
          .background(Color.Blue)
  )
}
```

If the UI of your app contains images, you should add content descriptions for them in most cases. Content descriptions are used, for example, by accessibility software to describe to visually impaired people what is currently presented on screen. So, by adding them, you greatly enhance the usability. Additionally, content descriptions help in finding composables. You can see these being used in the following code snippet:

```
@RunWith(AndroidJUnit4::class)
class AnotherInstrumentedTest {

    @get:Rule
    val rule = createComposeRule()

    @Test
    fun testImage() {
        var contentDescription = ""
        rule.setContent {
            ImageDemo()
            contentDescription = stringResource(id =
                R.string.airport_shuttle)
        }
        rule.onNodeWithContentDescription(contentDescription)
            .assertWidthIsEqualTo(128.dp)
    }
}
```

testImage() first sets the content (ImageDemo()). It then finds a semantics node with the given content description. Finally, assertWidthIsEqualTo() checks if the width of the UI element represented by this node is 128 density-independent pixels wide.

> **Tip**
>
> Have you noticed that I used `stringResource()` to obtain the content
> description? Hardcoded values can lead to subtle bugs in tests (for example,
> spelling errors or typos). To avoid them, try to write your tests in a way that
> they access the same values as the code being tested. But please keep in mind
> that under the hood, `stringResource()` relies on Android resources. So,
> the test case is platform-specific.

Using `onNodeWithText()` and `onNodeWithContentDescription()` makes it easy
to find composable functions that contain texts and images. But what if you need to find
the semantics node for something else—for example, a `Box()`? The following example,
`BoxButtonDemo()`, shows a `Box()` with a `Button()` centered inside. Clicking the
button toggles the background color of the box from white to light gray and back:

```
val COLOR1 = Color.White
val COLOR2 = Color.LightGray


@Composable
fun BoxButtonDemo() {
  var color by remember { mutableStateOf(COLOR1) }
  Box(
    modifier = Modifier
      .fillMaxSize()
      .background(color = color),
    contentAlignment = Alignment.Center
  ) {
    Button(onClick = {
      color = if (color == COLOR1)
        COLOR2
      else
        COLOR1
    }) {
      Text(text = stringResource(id = R.string.toggle))
    }
  }
}
```

Testing `BoxButtonDemo()` means finding the box, checking its initial background color, clicking the button, and checking the color again. To be able to find the box, we tag it using the `testTag()` modifier, as illustrated in the following code snippet. Applying a tag allows us to find the modified element in tests:

```
val TAG1 = "BoxButtonDemo"

Box(
  modifier = ...
    .testTag(TAG1)

  ...
```

We can check if the box is present, as follows:

```
@Test
fun testBoxInitialBackgroundColorIsColor1() {
  rule.setContent {
    BoxButtonDemo()
  }
  rule.onNode(hasTestTag(TAG1)).assertExists()
}
```

The `onNode()` finder receives a `hasTestTag()` **matcher**. Matchers find nodes that meet certain criteria. `hasTestTag()` finds a node with the given test tag. There are several predefined matchers. For example, `isEnabled()` returns whether the node is enabled, and `isToggleable()` returns `true` if the node can be toggled.

> **Tip**
>
> Google provides a testing cheat sheet at `https://developer.android.com/jetpack/compose/testing-cheatsheet`. It nicely groups finders, matchers, actions, and assertions.

To complete the code for the test, we need to check the background color of the box. But how do we do that? Following previous examples, you may expect a `hasBackgroundColor()` matcher. Unfortunately, there currently is none. Tests can rely only on what is available through the semantics tree, yet if it does not contain the information we need, we can easily add it. I will show you how in the following section.

Adding custom semantics properties

If you want to expose additional information to tests, you can create custom semantics properties. This requires the following:

- Defining `SemanticsPropertyKey`
- Making it available using `SemanticsPropertyReceiver`

You can see these in use in the following code snippet:

```
val BackgroundColorKey =
        SemanticsPropertyKey<Color>("BackgroundColor")
var SemanticsPropertyReceiver.backgroundColor by
 BackgroundColorKey


@Composable
fun BoxButtonDemo() {
  ...
  Box(
    modifier = ...
        .semantics { backgroundColor = color }
        .background(color = color),
    ...
```

With `SemanticsPropertyKey`, you can set key-value pairs in semantics blocks in a type-safe way. Each key has one statically defined value type—in my example, this is `Color`. `SemanticsPropertyReceiver` is the scope provided by `semantics {}` blocks. It is intended for setting key-value pairs via extension functions.

Here's how to access the custom semantic property in a test case:

```
@Test
fun testBoxInitialBackgroundColorIsColor1() {
  rule.setContent {
    BoxButtonDemo()
  }
  rule.onNode(SemanticsMatcher.expectValue
```

```
                    (BackgroundColorKey,COLOR1))
        .assertExists()
}
```

`expectValue()` checks whether the value of the given key is equal to the expected value.

Adding custom values to the semantics tree can be of great help when writing tests. However, please carefully consider if you really need to rely on `SemanticsPropertyKey`. The semantics tree is also used by the accessibility framework and tools, so it is vital to not pollute the semantics tree with irrelevant information. A solution is to rethink the testing strategy. Instead of testing *if the initial background color of the box is white*, we may just test if the value we pass to the `background()` function represents white.

This concludes the sections on testing composable functions. In the following section, we look at debugging Compose apps.

Debugging Compose apps

The title of this section, *Debugging Compose apps*, may indicate major differences to debugging traditional View-based apps. Fortunately, this is not the case. On Android, all composable hierarchies are wrapped inside `androidx.compose.ui.platform.ComposeView`. This happens indirectly if you invoke the `setContent {}` extension function of `ComponentActivity`, or if you deliberately include a composable hierarchy inside a layout (see *Chapter 9, Exploring Interoperability APIs*). Either way, in the end, `ComposeView` is displayed on screen—for example, inside an Activity or a Fragment. Therefore, all aspects regarding the basic building blocks of an Android app (Activities, Fragments, Services, Broadcast Receiver, Intents, and Content Provider) remain the same.

Of course, any UI framework advocates specific debugging habits. For example, the View system requires watching for `null` references. Also, you need to make sure that changes in state reliably trigger updates of the component tree. Fortunately, neither is relevant for Jetpack Compose. As composables are Kotlin functions, you can follow the creation of the composable hierarchy by stepping through the code and examining `State` when needed.

To closely examine the visual representation of your composable functions during runtime, you can use the **Layout Inspector** of Android Studio, as illustrated in the following screenshot. Once you have deployed your app on the Emulator or a real device, open the tool with **Layout Inspector** in the **Tools** menu:

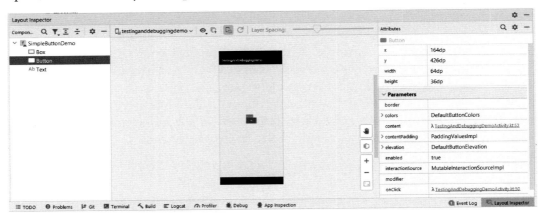

Figure 10.6 – The Layout Inspector in Android Studio

You can select the composable to inspect using the tree on the left-hand side of the Android Studio main window. Important attributes are presented on the right. The center of the tool window contains a configurable, zoomable preview. You can also enable a **three-dimensional** (**3D**) mode. This allows you to visually inspect the hierarchy by clicking and dragging to rotate the layout.

If you want to log important values of a composable for debugging purposes, you can easily achieve this with modifiers. The following section shows you how to do this.

Using custom modifiers for logging and debugging

As I explained in the *Modifying behavior* section of *Chapter 3*, *Exploring the Key Principles of Compose*, a modifier is an ordered, immutable collection of modifier elements. Modifiers can change the look and behavior of Compose UI elements. You create custom modifiers by implementing an extension function of `Modifier`. The following code snippet uses the `DrawScope` interface to print the size of a composable:

```
fun Modifier.simpleDebug() = then(object : DrawModifier {
  override fun ContentDrawScope.draw() {
    println("width=${size.width}, height=${size.height}")
    drawContent()
  }
})
```

Depending on which interface you choose, you can log different aspects. Using
LayoutModifier you could, for example, access layout-related information.

Important Note

While this may be a clever trick, it is certainly not the primary use case for
modifiers. Therefore, if you implement a custom modifier merely for debugging
purposes, you should add it to the modifier chain only when debugging.

There is also a built-in feature to provide additional information for debugging purposes.
Several modifiers can receive an inspectorInfo parameter, which is an extension
function of InspectorInfo. This class is a builder for an InspectableValue
interface (this interface defines a value that is inspectable by tools, giving access to private
parts of a value). InspectorInfo has three properties, as follows:

- name (provides nameFallback for InspectableValue)
- value (provides valueOverride for InspectableValue)
- properties (provides inspectableElements for InspectableValue)

To understand how inspectorInfo is used, let's look in the following screenshot at the
implementation of the semantics {} modifier, which adds semantics key-value pairs
for testing and accessibility. Please refer to the *Adding custom semantics properties* section
for details:

```
107    fun Modifier.semantics(
108        mergeDescendants: Boolean = false,
109        properties: (SemanticsPropertyReceiver.() → Unit)
110    ): Modifier = composed(
111        inspectorInfo = debugInspectorInfo {  this: InspectorInfo
112            name = "semantics"
113            this.properties["mergeDescendants"] = mergeDescendants
114            this.properties["properties"] = properties
115        }
116    ) {  this: Modifier
117        val id = remember { SemanticsModifierCore.generateSemanticsId() }
118        SemanticsModifierCore(id, mergeDescendants, clearAndSetSemantics = false, properties)
119    }
```

Figure 10.7 – Source code of the semantics {} modifier

semantics {} invokes the composed {} modifier, which receives two parameters,
inspectorInfo and factory (the modifier to be composed). The inspectorInfo
parameter gets the result of the debugInspectorInfo {} factory method (which
receives a name instance and two elements for properties as parameters).

composed {} adds a ComposedModifier class to the modifier chain. This private class implements the Modifier.Element interface and extends InspectorValueInfo, which in turn implements InspectorValueInfo. The inspectableElements property keeps Sequence of ValueElements.

To turn on debug inspector information, you must set the isDebugInspectorInfoEnabled global top-level variable in the androidx.compose.ui.platform package to true. Then, you can access and print debug inspector information using reflection. Here's the code you'll need:

```
.semantics { backgroundColor = color }.also {
    (it as CombinedModifier).run {
        val inner = this.javaClass.getDeclaredField("inner")
        inner.isAccessible = true
        val value = inner.get(this) as InspectorValueInfo
        value.inspectableElements.forEach {
            println(it)
        }
    }
}
```

The modifier returned by semantics {} is of type CombinedModifier because composed {} invokes then(), which uses CombinedModifier under the hood. Instead of just printing the raw inspectable element, you can customize the output to your needs.

Summary

In this chapter, we looked at important terms and techniques regarding testing. In the first main section, we set up the infrastructure, wrote and ran a simple unit test locally on the development machine, and then turned to Compose specifics. I introduced you to createComposeRule() and createAndroidComposeRule().

Next, we looked at how composable functions are found in a Compose hierarchy, and why making your app accessible also helps in writing better tests. You also learned about actions and assertions. Finally, we added custom entries to the semantics tree.

The final main section explained how to debug a Compose app. We revisited the semantics tree, and I showed you how to take advantage of InspectorInfo and InspectorValueInfo to debug custom modifiers.

Chapter 11, Conclusion and Next Steps, concludes this book. We look in the crystal ball to see what future versions of Jetpack Compose may add. For example, we preview Material 3 for Compose, which brings *Material You* design concepts to Compose apps. And we look beyond Android and examine Compose on other platforms.

Further reading

- This book assumes a basic understanding of how to test Android apps. To learn more, please refer to *Test apps on Android* at `https://developer.android.com/training/testing`.

- *JUnit in Action* by *Catalin Tudose* (*Manning Publications, 2020, ISBN 978-1617297045*) is a thorough introduction to the latest version of the JUnit testing framework.

- If you want to learn more about test automation, you may want to look at *Complete Guide to Test Automation: Techniques, Practices, and Patterns for Building and Maintaining Effective Software Projects* by *Arnon Axelrod* (*Apress, 2018, ISBN 978-1484238318*).

- To get an insight into the test pyramid metaphor, you may want to refer to *The Practical Test Pyramid* by *Ham Vocke*, available at `https://martinfowler.com/articles/practical-test-pyramid.html`.

11
Conclusion and Next Steps

This book shows you how to write beautiful, fast, and maintainable Jetpack Compose apps. In Chapters 1 to 3, I introduced you to the fundamentals of Jetpack Compose, explained core techniques and principles, as well as important interfaces, classes, packages, and, of course, composable functions. Chapters 4 to 7 focused on building Compose UIs. You learned how to manage state and navigate to different screens. We also explored the ViewModel and Repository patterns. Chapters 8 to 10 covered advanced topics such as animation, interoperability, testing, and debugging.

This final chapter is all about what you can do next. We'll investigate the near future of Jetpack Compose and explore neighboring platforms, because you can apply your Compose knowledge there, too. The main sections of this chapter are the following:

- Exploring the future
- Migrating to Material You
- Moving beyond Android

We'll start by looking at the next version of Jetpack Compose, 1.1, which was not yet stable when this book went into production. This iteration will bring bug fixes, performance improvements, and new features, for example, `ExposedDropdownMenuBox()`, an exposed drop-down menu, and `NavigationRail()`. This vertical navigation bar is intended for foldables and large-screen devices.

The second main section, *Migrating to Material You*, introduces you to Material 3 for Compose. This package contains *Material You*, the latest iteration of Google's beautiful design language, to Jetpack Compose apps. We'll look at some differences between Material 2 and Material 3, for example, the simplified typography and color schemes.

The *Moving beyond Android* section shows you how to use your Jetpack Compose knowledge on other platforms, for example, desktop and the web. I will briefly explain how to bring one of my sample composable functions to desktop.

Technical requirements

This chapter is based on the `ExposedDropdownMenuBoxDemo` and `NavigationRailDemo` samples. Please refer to the *Technical requirements* section in *Chapter 1*, *Building Your First Compose App*, for information about how to install and set up Android Studio, and how to get the repository accompanying this book.

All the code files for this chapter can be found on GitHub at `https://github.com/PacktPublishing/Android-UI-Development-with-Jetpack-Compose/tree/main/chapter_11`.

Exploring the future

This book is based on Jetpack Compose 1.0, the first stable version of the library, which was released in July 2021. Just like all other Jetpack components, Google is constantly enhancing and updating Compose. At the time of finishing the manuscript, version 1.1 was in beta. When it becomes stable, I will update the repository accompanying this book to reflect the changes. You can find the latest version of the samples of this book at `https://github.com/PacktPublishing/Android-UI-Development-with-Jetpack-Compose`.

Jetpack Compose 1.1 will offer bug fixes, new functionality, and performance improvements. New features include the following:

- The Compose compiler will support older versions of the Compose runtime. This allows you to use the latest tooling while still targeting older Compose versions.

- Touch target sizing (UI elements may get extra spacing to make them more accessible).

- `ImageVector` caching.
- Support for Android 12 stretch overscroll.

Several previously experimental APIs (for example, `AnimatedVisibility`, `EnterTransition`, and `ExitTransition`) will become stable. Additionally, Jetpack Compose 1.1 will support newer versions of Kotlin. Unfortunately, you will also face some breaking changes. For example, lambdas in `EnterTransition` and `ExitTransition` factories may be moved to the last position in the parameter list.

Showing exposed drop-down menus

There are also new Material UI elements. For example, `ExposedDropdownMenuBox()` shows an exposed drop-down menu, which displays the currently selected menu item above the list of options. The `ExposedDropdownMenuBoxDemo` sample illustrates the usage of the composable function (*Figure 11.1*).

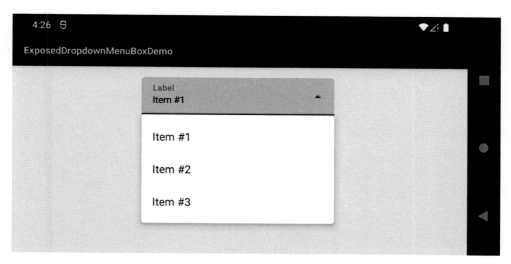

Figure 11.1 – The ExposedDropdownMenuBoxDemo sample

Currently, `ExposedDropdownMenuBox()` is marked experimental. Therefore, you must add the `@ExperimentalMaterialApi` annotation:

```
@ExperimentalMaterialApi
@Composable
fun ExposedDropdownMenuBoxDemo() {
  val titles = List(3) { i ->
    stringResource(id = R.string.item, i + 1)
```

```
    }
    var expanded by remember { mutableStateOf(false) }
    var selectedTxt by remember { mutableStateOf(titles[0]) }
    Box(
      modifier = Modifier
        .fillMaxSize()
        .padding(16.dp),
      contentAlignment = Alignment.TopCenter
    ) {
      ...
    }
  }
}
```

ExposedDropdownMenuBoxDemo() puts ExposedDropdownMenuBox() in a Box() and horizontally centers the menu at the top. The menu items are stored in a list (titles). The expanded state reflects the visibility of the menu items. selectedTxt represents the currently selected text. Here's how they are used:

```
ExposedDropdownMenuBox(expanded = expanded,
  onExpandedChange = {
    expanded = !expanded
  }) {
  TextField(value = selectedTxt,
    onValueChange = { },
    readOnly = true,
    label = {
      Text(text = stringResource(id = R.string.label))
    },
    trailingIcon = {
      ExposedDropdownMenuDefaults.TrailingIcon(
        expanded = expanded
      )
    }
  )
  ExposedDropdownMenu(expanded = expanded,
    onDismissRequest = {
```

```
        expanded = false
    }) {
    for (title in titles) {
        DropdownMenuItem(onClick = {
            expanded = false
            selectedTxt = title
        }) {
            Text(text = title)
        }
    }
    }
}
```

ExposedDropdownMenuBox() has two children, read-only TextField() and ExposedDropdownMenu(). The text field shows selectedTxt. As readOnly is set to true, the onValueChange block can be empty. expanded controls the trailing icon, which reflects the visibility of the menu items. The onExpandedChange lambda expression passed to ExposedDropdownMenuBox() is executed when the user clicks on the exposed drop-down menu. Usually, you will negate expanded.

ExposedDropdownMenu() has at least one DropdownMenuItem() as its content. Typically, you will want to hide the menu (expanded = false) and update the text field (selectedTxt = title). The onDismissRequest block passed to ExposedDropdownMenu() should also close the menu, but not update the text field.

So, ExposedDropdownMenuBox() is a very compact way of showing a selection of items and allowing the user to choose one. In the following section, I show you another Material UI element that debuts in Compose 1.1. NavigationRail() presents top-level navigation destinations vertically.

Using NavigationRail()

Compose offers several ways to navigate to top-level destinations within your app. For example, you can place a navigation bar at the bottom of the screen using BottomNavigation(). I show you how to use it in the *Adding navigation* section of *Chapter 6, Putting Pieces Together*. Jetpack Compose 1.1 includes another UI element for top-level navigation. NavigationRail() implements the **navigation rail** interaction pattern, a vertical navigation bar especially for large screens such as tablets and open foldables.

If the screen is not big enough, or the foldable is closed, a standard bottom navigation bar should be displayed instead. The `NavigationRailDemo` sample shows how to achieve this. In *Figure 11.2*, you can see the app in portrait mode.

#1

Figure 11.2 – The NavigationRailDemo sample in portrait mode

To continue, an elaborate approach would be to use the Jetpack `WindowManager` library, however this is beyond the scope of the book. Instead, we will use `NavigationRailDemo ( )` for the sake of simplicity, which determines whether the navigation rail should be used by simply comparing the current width of the screen with the minimum size (600 density-independent pixels):

```
@Composable
fun NavigationRailDemo() {
    val showNavigationRail =
            LocalConfiguration.current.screenWidthDp >= 600
    val index = rememberSaveable { mutableStateOf(0) }
    Scaffold(topBar = {
        TopAppBar(title = {
            Text(text = stringResource(id = R.string.app_name))
        })
    },
```

```
    bottomBar = {
        if (!showNavigationRail)
            BottomBar(index)
    }) {
        Content(showNavigationRail, index)
    }
}
```

Scaffold() receives bottom bars through the bottomBar lambda expression.
If the navigation rail should not be shown (showNavigationRail is false), my
BottomBar() composable is invoked. Otherwise, no bottom bar is added. The currently
active screen is stored in a mutable Int state (index). It is passed to BottomBar() and
Content(). Next, let's briefly revisit how BottomNavigation() works by looking at
my BottomBar() composable:

```
@Composable
fun BottomBar(index: MutableState<Int>) {
    BottomNavigation {
        for (i in 0..2)
            BottomNavigationItem(selected = i == index.value,
                onClick = { index.value = i },
                icon = {
                    Icon(
                        painter = painterResource(id =
                            R.drawable.ic_baseline_android_24),
                        contentDescription = null
                    )
                },
                label = {
                    MyText(index = i)
                }
            )
    }
}
```

The content of `BottomNavigation()` consists of several `BottomNavigationItem()` elements with an icon, a label, and an `onClick` block. My implementation just updates the `index` state, which is also used inside `Content()`. This composable displays the navigation rail if needed, and the main content (screen), which is just a box with text centered inside:

```kotlin
@Composable
fun Content(showNavigationRail: Boolean, index:
    MutableState<Int>) {
  Row(
    modifier = Modifier.fillMaxSize()
  ) {
    if (showNavigationRail) {
      NavigationRail {
        for (i in 0..2)
          NavigationRailItem(selected = i == index.value,
            onClick = {
              index.value = i
            },
            icon = {
              Icon(
                painter = painterResource(id =
                    R.drawable.ic_baseline_android_24),
                contentDescription = null
              )
            },
            label = {
              MyText(index = i)
            })
      }
    }
    Box(
      modifier = Modifier
        .fillMaxSize()
        .background(color = MaterialTheme.colors.surface),
      contentAlignment = Alignment.Center
    ) {
```

```
MyText (
    index = index.value,
    style = MaterialTheme.typography.h3
    )
  }
 }
}
```

The navigation rail and the screen are arranged horizontally in `Row()`. Like `BottomNavigation()`, `NavigationRail()` gets one or more child elements that represent the navigation destinations. The children (`NavigationRailItem()`) have a label, an icon, and an `onClick` block. *Figure 11.3* shows the `NavigationRailDemo` sample in landscape mode.

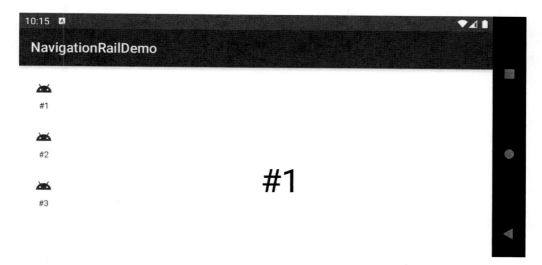

Figure 11.3 – The NavigationRailDemo sample in landscape mode

While Jetpack Compose 1.1 will add some Material UI elements and polish the existing ones, it still implements *Material Design* as present in previous Android versions, including 11 (sometimes referred to as Material 2). *Material You*, which debuted with Android 12, will be available for Compose, too. However, it is not an in-place update of the existing packages but comes as a new library. In the following section, we look at Material 3 for Jetpack Compose, which was in early alpha at the time this chapter was written.

> **Note**
>
> You may be wondering what the difference between Material You and Material 3 is. I am referring to Material 3 as the latest version of the Material Design specification, whereas Material You is the implementation on Android 12.

Migrating to Material You

Material You is the latest iteration of Google's design language Material Design. It was announced during Google I/O 2021 and was first available on Pixel smartphones running Android 12. Eventually, it will be rolled out to other devices, form factors, and frameworks. Like its predecessors, Material You is based on typography, animation, and layers. But it emphasizes personalization: depending on the platform, *Material You* implementations may use color palettes derived from the system wallpaper.

Looking at some differences between Material 2 and Material 3 for Compose

To use *Material You* in your Compose app, you must add an implementation dependency to `androidx.compose.material3:material3` in the module-level `build.gradle` file. The base package for composables, classes, and interfaces changes to `androidx.compose.material3`. If you want to migrate an existing Compose app to this new version, you at least need to change imports. Unfortunately, the names of quite a few composable functions will change, too. To get an idea of the differences, I have reimplemented `NavigationRailDemo` for *Material You*. The project is named `NavigationRailDemo_Material3`. This way, you can easily examine the changes by comparing important files.

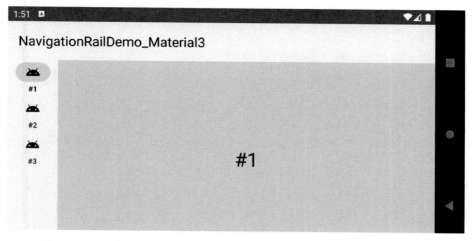

Figure 11.4 – The NavigationRailDemo_Material3 sample in landscape mode

Specifically, `TopAppBar()` needs to be replaced by `SmallTopAppBar()` or one of its bigger siblings, `MediumTopAppBar()` and `LargeTopAppBar()`. Other changes include the following:

- `BottomNavigation()` will be generalized to `NavigationBar()`.
- `BottomNavigationItem()` is now called `NavigationBarItem()`.
- `NavigationRailItem()` remains unchanged.

The last bullet point is interesting: as `NavigationRailItem()` elements very much resemble `NavigationBarItem()`, I wonder if these two may be generalized in the future.

Several properties that control the visual representation of UI elements will change considerably. For example, Material colors belong to `MaterialTheme.colorScheme` instead of the former `MaterialTheme.colors`. For more information about colors in Material 3, please refer to the official documentation at `https://m3.material.io/styles/color/dynamic-color/overview`.

Styled texts may also require some adaptions because the members of the `Typography` class will be simplified. For example, instead of h1, h2, h3, and so on, you will use `headlineLarge`, `headlineMedium`, or `headlineSmall`.

This concludes our brief look at the changes regarding Material 3 and the near future of Jetpack Compose. Did you know you can write Compose apps for the web and desktop, too? In the following section, we give it a try.

Moving beyond Android

While Jetpack Compose is the new UI toolkit on Android, its underlying ideas and principles make it attractive for other platforms, too. Let's see why this is the case:

1. The declarative approach was first implemented on the web.

2. SwiftUI, Apple's implementation of a declarative UI framework, works well for iPhones, iPads, watches, and macOS devices.

3. Jetpack Compose UI elements use Material Design, which is designed for different platforms, device categories, and form factors.

Most importantly, core concepts such as state and composable functions are not Android-specific. Therefore, if someone provides the toolchain (for example, the Kotlin compiler and the Compose compiler), any platform capable of showing graphics *may* be able to execute Compose apps. Certainly, there is an awful lot of work to be done.

For example, the Compose UI must be hosted *somewhere*. On Android, activities are used. On the web, this would be a browser window. And on desktop, it would be a window provided by some UI toolkit. Any other functionality (for example, network and file I/O, connectivity, memory management, threading) must be addressed by other libraries or frameworks.

JetBrains, the inventor of Kotlin and IntelliJ, decided to tackle this. In recent years, the company gained a lot of experience in targeting multiple platforms and sharing code among them. For example, with *Kotlin Multiplatform Mobile* you can use a single code base for the business logic of iOS and Android apps. *Compose Multiplatform* aims to simplify and speed up the development of UIs for desktop and the web, and to share UI code among them and Android.

In the following section, I will briefly show how to create a simple Compose for Desktop application using the IntelliJ IDE.

Setting up a sample project

The easiest way to create a Compose for Desktop project is to use the project wizard of the IntelliJ IDE. This requires IntelliJ IDEA Community Edition or Ultimate Edition 2020.3 or later. Setting up IntelliJ is beyond the scope of this book and is not detailed here. *Figure 11.5* shows you how to fill in the project wizard dialog.

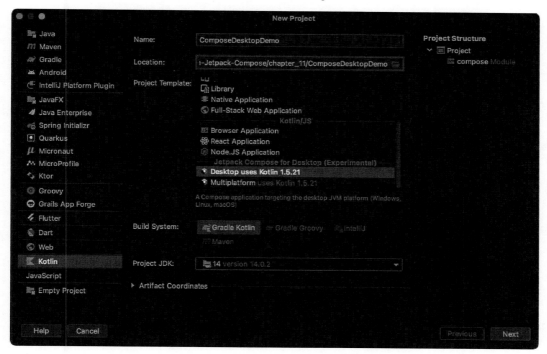

Figure 11.5 – The IntelliJ project wizard

JetBrains maintains a *Getting started with Compose Multiplatform* tutorial on GitHub at `https://github.com/JetBrains/compose-jb/blob/master/tutorials/Getting_Started/README.md`. Please refer to this for additional information.

The project wizard adds a simple `Main.kt` file inside `src/main/kotlin`. You can run it from the **Gradle** tool window by double-clicking on **Tasks | compose desktop | run** (*Figure 11.6*).

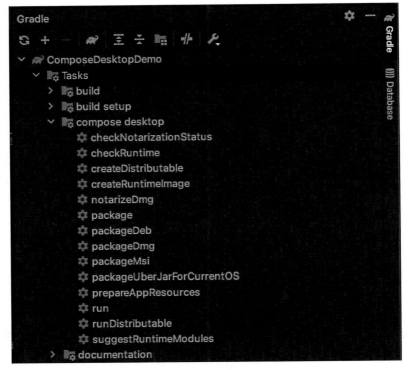

Figure 11.6 – The IntelliJ Gradle tool window

The source code contains a composable called `App()`. It is invoked from the `main()` function. Let's replace the body of `App()` with one of my samples, for example, `StateChangeDemo()` from *Chapter 8, Working with Animations*:

```kotlin
@Composable
@Preview
fun App() {
  var toggled by remember {
    mutableStateOf(false)
  }
  val color = if (toggled)
    Color.White
  else
```

```
      Color.Red
   Column(
      modifier = Modifier
         .fillMaxSize()
         .padding(16.dp),
      horizontalAlignment = Alignment.CenterHorizontally
   ) {
      Button(onClick = {
         toggled = !toggled
      }) {
         Text(text = "Toggle")
      }
      Box(
         modifier = Modifier
            .padding(top = 32.dp)
            .background(color = color)
            .size(128.dp)
      )
   }
}
```

Have you noticed that I changed one line? The original version uses the
stringResource() composable. However, Android resources are not available
on desktop so you must replace the invocation with something different. A simple
workaround is to hardcode the text. Real-world applications may want to choose
a mechanism that supports multiple languages. Compose for Desktop relies on the Java
Virtual Machine, so you can use Java's internationalization support.

The app running on macOS is shown in *Figure 11.7*.

Figure 11.7 – A simple Compose for Desktop app

This concludes our brief look at Compose for Desktop and Compose Multiplatform. To learn more, please visit the product page at `https://www.jetbrains.com/de-de/lp/compose-mpp/`.

Summary

In this final chapter, we looked at the near future of Jetpack Compose and glimpsed neighboring platforms. Jetpack Compose 1.1 will bring bug fixes, performance improvements, and new features, for example, `ExposedDropdownMenuBox()` and `NavigationRail()`. Two samples (`ExposedDropdownMenuBoxDemo` and `NavigationRailDemo`) show you how to use them.

The second main section, *Migrating to Material You*, introduced you to Material 3 for Compose. This package brings *Material You*, the latest iteration of Google's beautiful design language, to Jetpack Compose apps. We looked at some differences between Material 2 and Material 3, for example, the simplified typography and color schemes.

Moving beyond Android showed you how to use your Jetpack Compose knowledge on another platform. I explained how to bring one of my sample composable functions to desktop.

I sincerely hope you enjoyed reading this book. You now have a thorough understanding of the core principles of Jetpack Compose, as well as the important advantages over the traditional Android View system. Using a declarative approach makes writing great-looking apps easier than ever. I can't wait to see which beautiful ideas you are going to turn into code.

Index

Packt.com

Subscribe to our online digital library for full access to over 7,000 books and videos, as well as industry leading tools to help you plan your personal development and advance your career. For more information, please visit our website.

Why subscribe?

- Spend less time learning and more time coding with practical eBooks and Videos from over 4,000 industry professionals

- Improve your learning with Skill Plans built especially for you

- Get a free eBook or video every month

- Fully searchable for easy access to vital information

- Copy and paste, print, and bookmark content

Did you know that Packt offers eBook versions of every book published, with PDF and ePub files available? You can upgrade to the eBook version at packt.com and as a print book customer, you are entitled to a discount on the eBook copy. Get in touch with us at customercare@packtpub.com for more details.

At www.packt.com, you can also read a collection of free technical articles, sign up for a range of free newsletters, and receive exclusive discounts and offers on Packt books and eBooks.

Other Books You May Enjoy

If you enjoyed this book, you may be interested in these other books by Packt:

Mastering Kotlin

Nate Ebel

ISBN: 978-1-83855-572-6

- Model data using interfaces, classes, and data classes
- Grapple with practical interoperability challenges and solutions with Java
- Build parallel apps using concurrency solutions such as coroutines
- Explore functional, reactive, and imperative programming to build flexible apps
- Discover how to build your own domain-specific language
- Embrace functional programming using the standard library and Arrow
- Delve into the use of Kotlin for frontend JavaScript development
- Build server-side services using Kotlin and Ktor

Android Programming with Kotlin for Beginners

John Horton

ISBN: 978-1-78961-540-1

- Learn how Kotlin and Android work together
- Build a graphical drawing app using Object-Oriented Programming (OOP) principles
- Build beautiful, practical layouts using ScrollView, RecyclerView, NavigationView, ViewPager and CardView
- Write Kotlin code to manage an apps' data using different strategies including JSON and the built-in Android SQLite database
- Add user interaction, data captures, sound, and animation to your apps
- Implement dialog boxes to capture input from the user
- Build a simple database app that sorts and stores the user's data

Packt is searching for authors like you

If you're interested in becoming an author for Packt, please visit authors.packtpub.com and apply today. We have worked with thousands of developers and tech professionals, just like you, to help them share their insight with the global tech community. You can make a general application, apply for a specific hot topic that we are recruiting an author for, or submit your own idea.

Share Your Thoughts

Now you've finished *Android UI Development with Jetpack Compose*, we'd love to hear your thoughts! Scan the QR code below to go straight to the Amazon review page for this book and share your feedback or leave a review on the site that you purchased it from.

https://www.amazon.in/review/create-review/error?asin=1801812160

Your review is important to us and the tech community and will help us make sure we're delivering excellent quality content.

Made in the USA
Las Vegas, NV
27 March 2022

46406080R10150